W9-BUM-610

POPULATION and the JAPANESE ECONOMY

JAPAN LIBRARY

Longevity, Innovation, and Economic Growth

YOSHIKAWA Hiroshi

Translated by Charles Stewart

Japan Publishing Industry Foundation for Culture

NOTE TO READERS

This book follows the Hepburn system of romanization. In general, Japanese names are given in Japanese order (surname first) for persons active before the Meiji Restoration of 1868, and in Western order (surname last) for persons active after that. Macrons are used in people's and place names, except very common place names such as "Tokyo."

Population and the Japanese Economy: Longevity, Innovation, and Economic Growth
Yoshikawa Hiroshi. Translated by Charles Stewart.

Published by
Japan Publishing Industry Foundation for Culture (JPIC)
2-2-30 Kanda-Jinbocho, Chiyoda-ku, Tokyo 101-0051, Japan

First English edition: March 2020

This book is a translation of *Jinkō to Nihon keizai: Chōju, inobēshon, keizai seichō* (Chuokoron-Shinsha, Inc., 2016).
English publishing rights arranged with the author.

Jacket and cover design: Miki Kazuhiko, Ampersand Works

Printed in Japan
ISBN 978-4-86658-056-2
https://japanlibrary.jpic.or.jp/

To Ritsu, our grandson, who will live to see the twenty-second century.

Contents

CHAPTER 3 The Fruit Called Longevity..................107

CHAPTER 4 What Does Economics Mean for People? 147

Preface to the English edition

This is the English edition of my book *Jinkō to Nihon keizai*, which was published by Chuokoron Shinsha in 2016. Fortunately, it was widely read and discussed in Japan, and has been translated into Chinese and Korean. Now, JPIC has kindly translated it into English. Declining population and aging are certainly the most important problems facing Japan and many other countries in the world today.

In Japan, despite wide public attention and policy efforts made by the government, the trend has not stopped; rather, it appears to be accelerating. After World War II, between 1947 and 1949, 2.6 million babies were born, a phenomenon that became known as the postwar baby boom. Only 918,000 babies were born in 2018, a historical low in modern times. The fertility rate—that is, the average number of babies a woman bears in her lifetime—remained at 1.42 in 2018, far below the government's target. Meanwhile, the average life expectancy continues to rise, reaching an average of 81.25 for males and 87.32 for females in 2018. There are now 71,000 people aged 100 and older in Japan. Furthermore, Japan's population declined by 444,000 in 2018, dropping by more than 400,000 for the first time.

This book is about population and the economy, drawing on Japan's experiences as a reference. I hope that it is of interest to people outside Japan.

I would like to thank Mr. Charles Stewart for his excellent translation, and Messrs. Kiyoshi Nakaizumi and Izumi Ozaki of JPIC for this project.

October 11, 2019
Hiroshi Yoshikawa

Preface

When the "bubble economy" collapsed at the beginning of the 1990s, Japan entered a long tunnel. Although there is more than one reason for the sense of hopelessness that has persisted over the quarter-century since that time, the shrinking population is always cited as a negative factor.

The purpose of this book is to consider population—which is a key word when thinking about twenty-first-century Japan, or for that matter the world—in connection with economics. Population might be called the final outcome of human history. Population phenomena are complex and cannot be elucidated in their entirety by any single existing field of study. This book is simply an essay on the relationship between economics and population.

During the eighteenth century, Europe, where economics was established as an emerging discipline, was undergoing a population explosion. Naturally, Adam Smith and the other economists of the day developed a lively discourse regarding population. Particularly famous among these is *An Essay on the Principle of Population* by Robert Malthus, which is invariably brought up when population is discussed. In chapter 1, after a simple review of the history of population, I introduce the arguments put forth by Malthus in the eighteenth century, along with those made by Keynes, also in England, who examined the impact of population decline on the economy in the first half of the twentieth century, and by the Swedish economists who pioneered efforts toward resolving the population problem ahead of other countries.

Since ancient times, there have been various arguments from opposing viewpoints that the population is "too large" or "too small." But in Japan today, the decline of the population is already causing many problems. The effects on social security, public finances, and regional communities are particularly serious. Such issues are investigated in chapter 2.

The decline of the population is definitely a grave issue. Nevertheless, the "population-decline pessimism" casting a pall over the Japanese economy has gone entirely too far. In the second half of chapter 2, I argue that what determines economic growth in industrialized nations is not population but innovation. While some people say that, because the working population is shrinking, economic growth will be impossible and we should expect zero growth at best, others are concerned conversely that more and more people will lose their places of work because of the development of AI (artificial intelligence). Such issues are also considered in chapter 2.

In Europe, the trend toward population decline became clear at the end of the nineteenth century. This violated Malthus' principle of population, which states that, when per capita income rises, the number of children increases and population grows. Ever since Charles Darwin, drawing inspiration from Malthus, published *On the Origin of Species*, the common assumption for the world of plants and animals, as well, has been that when food supply increases, the numbers of organisms also increase. In human society, however, population has declined in countries with high income levels. In parallel with this, there have been remarkable increases in life expectancy. Malthus vigorously disputed that possibility. When we speak of "inequality," one of the key words in the twenty-first century, inequalities of income and wealth come to mind, but in fact there is also inequality in life expectancy. The extension of life expectancy is closely related to innovation. Population decline and life expectancy are examined in chapter 3.

A factor that has a large impact on both population and life expectancy is per capita income—and it is innovation that bolsters per capita income. Innovation is the wellspring of economic growth in industrialized nations.

Having said that, is economic growth desirable to begin with? Is economic growth meaningful? This is a question that has been asked since ancient times. In economic circles, the "zero growth theory" of John Stuart Mill, the nineteenth-century intellectual giant, is well known. When this question is pursued to its end, it leads to the fundamental question of what economics means for people.

That is a question which twenty-first-century Japan and the world must answer; it is also the theme of chapter 4.

Economics and Population

For Japan, and for other countries including China, demographics is the greatest issue of the twenty-first century.

According to the "Population Projection for Japan" (medium fertility assumption) released by Japan's National Institute of Population and Social Security Research in January 2017, the population of Japan will be 50.5 million in the year 2115. Because Japan's population was 127.11 million in 2015 (*2015 Population Census of Japan*), this means Japan's population will decline to less than half its current level over the next 100 years. Such a huge change in population should certainly have a great effect on the economy and society of Japan. After all, population is the most fundamental piece of data for society.

In this chapter, I begin with a simple overview of how population has changed throughout history and then proceed with a review of how economics has viewed population.

The population of Japan

Let us start by examining the population of Japan. Many scholars have attempted to make estimates of the population of Japan since before World War II, applying expertise from anthropology and other fields.

One of these was Goichi Sawada, a remarkable academic in the Taishō era (1912–26) who was a pioneer in estimating the Japanese population. Sawada was a mathematician who graduated with a bachelor's degree from the department of physics at the University of Tokyo and worked as a professor at the Tokyo University of Commerce (now Hitotsubashi University). In 1920, when he was almost sixty years old, Sawada was readmitted to the University of Tokyo, received a bachelor of arts from the department of Japanese history, and devoted the rest of his life to estimating the population of Japan during the Nara period (710–94). Using such data as the number of taxpayers (males between seventeen and sixty-five years of age) per administrative village, the number of administrative villages nationwide, and the percentage of adult males in the total population, Sawada estimated that the population of Japan was 6 million during the Nara period. The figure of 4.51 million shown in chart 1-1 is lower than Sawada's estimate, but this probably reflects subsequent research.

At any rate, those figures are estimates made by subsequent generations some 1,200 years later. During the Nara period, the central government was able to determine the population of Japan in real time, but those records were unfortunately lost. Starting in the reign of Empress Jitō (686–97), household registers were recorded nationwide every six years with detailed information on each occupant including name, age, sex, and household relations. These were sent from the provincial governors to the Ministry of the Center and the Ministry of Internal Affairs in the central government. In addition to the household registers updated every six years, statistical documents called tax registers were prepared annually, and based on these, budgets were compiled by the budget examiners of the Ministry of Popular Affairs. Thus, during the Nara period a national census was conducted every six years via the household registers. In the ninth century, however, the household registers started being recorded every twelve years, and then once every few decades, and they were finally suspended altogether in the tenth century. That was followed by a long hiatus until the population surveys of the Edo period (1603–1868) and the modern census of the Meiji period (1868–1912). This history truly demonstrates how the Nara period was the peak of centralized administration in ancient Japan.

There are superb explications regarding the population of Japan by historical demography specialists. The changes in Japan's population are shown in chart 1-1, based on data from *Jinkō kara yomu Nihon no rekishi* (A view of Japanese history through population) by Hiroshi Kitō (2000).

Japan's population is believed to have greatly declined toward the end of the Jōmon period (14,000–300 B.C.), in part because the cooling of the climate reduced the quantity of fruits and nuts that could be harvested from deciduous trees. Looking at the times since the Nara period for which fragmentary records remain, along with periods of large population growth there have also been times when the population remained unchanged. For example, the population of Japan increased greatly for the first hundred years of the Edo period in the seventeenth century, but stopped growing in the eighteenth century; it remained stagnant from the Kyōhō era

(1716–36) of the eighth shogun Tokugawa Yoshimune through the last days of the Tokugawa shogunate in the mid-1800s.

The population of Japan began to grow again in the Meiji period, and at a pace so rapid it could be called explosive. Then, in 1920, the birthrate began to decline, starting in the urban areas. There was a temporary jump from 1947 to 1949, immediately after World War II—this was the emergence of the so-called baby-boom generation—but the rate of population growth rapidly diminished from 1975 onward. The

Chart 1-1. Changes in the Population of Japan

YEAR	PERIOD OR ERA	POPULATION
3200 B.C.*	Early Jōmon period	106,000
2300 B.C.	Middle Jōmon period	261,000
1300 B.C.	Late Jōmon period	160,000
900 B.C.	Final Jōmon period	76,000
200	Yayoi period	595,000
725	Nara period	4,512,000
1150	Late Heian period	6,837,000
1600	Keichō 5	12,273,000
1721	Kyōhō 6	31,279,000
1792	Kansei 4	29,870,000
1798	Kansei 10	30,565,000
1828	Bunsei 11	32,626,000
1834	Tenpō 5	32,477,000
1846	Kōka 3	32,297,000
1873	Meiji 6	33,301,000
1890	Meiji 23	41,309,000
1920	Taishō 9	55,963,000
1950	Shōwa 25	83,898,000
1975	Shōwa 50	111,940,000
1995	Heisei 7	125,570,000

*The era designation of B.P. used in the original source has been converted to B.C.
Source: Kitō 2000.

population of Japan peaked at 127,790,000 in 2004 and has been declining ever since.

There have been slight reductions in population in the past, but there has never been a decrease as drastic as the one we are about to experience, in which the population is expected to fall by half in a hundred-year period. We have entered an era of population decline that humanity has never experienced before.

The population of China

In both the East and the West, since ancient times, records of population have been kept wherever civilization developed. The population of China, now the world's largest at an estimated 1.37 billion, is not clearly known prior to the Qin dynasty (221–206 B.C.). However, China's population as early as the second year of the rule of Emperor Ping of the Western Han dynasty (2 A.D.) is recorded in the *Book of Han: Treatise on Geography*. The *Book of Han*, which was edited by Ban Gu, is the second-oldest official dynastic history, following Sima Qian's *Records of the Grand Historian*. The *Treatise on Geography* includes the oldest written record regarding Japan: "The people of Wa, who are located across the ocean from Lelang Commandery, are divided into more than one hundred tribes . . ." Every Japanese must recall seeing this in history textbooks. In the "Account of the Wa People," the famous *Book of Wei*, which describes life in the third century, mentions the ancient Japanese country Yamatai-koku that was ruled over by Queen Himiko. The *Book of Han* was written some 200 years earlier.

According to the *Book of Han*, in the year 2 A.D. there were 12,233,062 households in Han, and the population was 59,594,978. The household registers kept in Japan during the Nara period are mentioned above, but China already had household registers 700 years earlier and also conducted population surveys in August each year, which were called the *anbi* and the *suanren*. These were not performed out of curiosity but for the purpose of accurately levying a per capita tax called the *suanfu*. The Chinese Empire was concerned with population numbers beginning in ancient times, mostly because of the need for levying taxes and military conscription.

The transition of China's population is shown in chart 1-2 as derived by Katō (1944), who selected figures for various years from official histories starting with the *Book of Han: Treatise on Geography*. While we speak of "China" as a single entity, its geographical territory has changed over time and there is naturally room for some argument regarding the accuracy of the population figures in the official histories.

Chart 1-2. Changes in the Population of China

YEAR	DYNASTY, EMPEROR, ERA YEAR	POPULATION
2	Western Han, Emperor Ping, Yuanshi 2	59,594,978
57	Eastern Han, Emperor Guangwu, Zhogyuan 2	21,007,820
726	Tang, Emperor Xuanzong, Kaiyuan 14	41,419,712
1110	Song, Emperor Huizong, Daguan 4	46,734,784
1578	Ming, Emperor Shenzong, Wanli 6	60,692,856
1792	Qing, Emperor Gaozong, Qianlong 57	307,467,279

Source: Katō 1944.

This is still being researched by experts today. These figures are, nonetheless, sufficient for us to see the overall dynamics of the Chinese population.

In particular, even after considering the lack of precision in the statistics, the decrease in the Chinese population by about two-thirds during the roughly fifty years from 2 to 57 A.D. is conspicuous. This must have resulted from the massacres and starvation caused by civil wars during this time. In fact, in her "Poems of Grief and Resentment," the Chinese Poet Cai Yan, who lived during this period of chaos at the end of the Eastern Han dynasty, wrote in graphic detail about the social disorder of her time. Having been captured by non-Chinese people who lived in the north, she wrote upon finally returning to her country that northern China was in a terrible state. "There were bleached bones scattered everywhere, and no one could tell whose they were." Under such conditions, the population fell dramatically. There is no doubt that human history has known such times.

The population of China subsequently doubled over the next 650 years through the Tang dynasty (618–907), with an average population increase rate of over 0.1 percent per year. Over the 400 years from the Tang dynasty through the Song dynasty (960–1279), however, the population rose very slowly, at an average annual rate of less than 0.03 percent, according to the figures recorded in the official histories.

Konan Naitō, who is renowned as a great scholar of Oriental history, said that in dividing Chinese history into periods, the "modern" era began with the Song dynasty. Naitō notes that the Chinese economy began developing at that time, and argues that the conspicuous increase in the population was supported not only by the development of agricultural technologies but also by advances in methods of cooking that allowed almost anything to be eaten. This is the "Chinese food" that can be found all over the world today. In China, in addition to the exceptionally wide variety of foodstuffs, there was also unique ingenuity in the use of spices. Developments that can be compared to the use of Chinese herbs in the world of medicine were evident in Chinese cooking as well, and these supported population growth. Especially during the Song dynasty, the population growth in Jiang Nan, which had a vibrant economy, was particularly conspicuous. During the Northern Song dynasty, the population of China exceeded 100 million for the first time in history. It peaked in the 1210s during the Southern Song dynasty, and then began to decline (Ihara and Umemura 1997).

But China's population really entered a period of explosive growth during the last dynasty, which was the Qing dynasty, even after discounting for the expansion of Chinese territory. At the peak of the Qing dynasty, during the rule of the Qianlong emperor (1735–95), China became a population superpower with 300 million people. While agricultural production increased thanks in part to technological progress, it was the improvement in the people's livelihood from a reduction in the tax burden that sparked this population growth in China during the eighteenth century (Ho 1959).

Since the establishment of the People's Republic of China in 1949, China's population has rapidly increased once again. Aided by a decline in the mortality rate, in the thirty years through 1979 the population increased by 1.8 times, from 500 million to 900 million. Mao Zedong, who was the absolute leader at that time, viewed population as an indicator of national strength. As food production failed to keep pace with the population increase, however, the Chinese government imposed harsh population restrictions starting in 1979, including the "one-child policy." Despite these measures, China now has a population of 1.37 billion, which is the largest in the world.

After more than thirty years, China abolished its extreme "one-child policy" at the 2015 meeting of the Central Committee of the Communist Party of China. The background to this great reversal was the major issue of the shift from the "fast-growth" era, which saw annual economic growth of 10 percent, to a "new normal" of medium-fast economic growth at an annual rate of around 6 percent. Amid this decline in the economic growth rate, China is facing a rapid aging of its society in the twenty-first century. To achieve the target growth rate of 6 percent, the country must increase its working population; this is the reason for the policy change.

The world population

We have reviewed the population of Japan and its neighbor China, but how has the population of the entire world changed since the first humans emerged in Africa seven million years ago? The world population has grown overall throughout history. This can be broadly divided into three periods based on the rate of increase (Livi Bacci 2012).

First is the period from the birth of humanity—said to be around 7 million years ago—through the Paleolithic era. Naturally, the population during this time can only be roughly estimated, based on several assumptions. Nonetheless, the total world population from 35,000 B.C. through 30,000 B.C. never exceeded some hundreds of thousands, and the average annual growth rate is believed to have been less than 0.01 percent. While the population did increase, the pace was extremely gradual. It took a mind-numbing period of more than 8,000 years for the population to double.

A great change occurred with the arrival of the Neolithic era around 10,000 B.C. Neolithic stone implements enabled humans to fell large trees, and agriculture and stock breeding began. Humans, who had led a nomadic lifestyle of hunting and gathering up until that time, formed fixed settlements as they gained control of their own food supply through agriculture and animal husbandry. To put it in today's economic terms, the per capita income undoubtedly increased dramatically, and the population growth rate rose as a result. Surprisingly, however, one theory says the mortality rate also rose as a result of fixed settlement. As we will examine later on, urban areas with high population density were disadvantageous for human survival compared with rural areas until the start of the twentieth century. During the Neolithic era, the nomadic lifestyle may have had means of maintaining good hygienic conditions that made it more advantageous than fixed settlement. Yet even if it is a fact that the mortality rate rose from the fixed settlement of humanity during the Neolithic era, the birthrate rose by more than enough to make up for the higher mortality, so the population increased anyway. The average annual population growth rate rose to 0.04 percent, and at that pace the population doubled in less than 2,000 years. Consequently, the world population increased from about six million at the start of the Neolithic era, around 10,000 B.C., to 250 million around the year 1 A.D. However, one feels mixed emotions upon learning that the average life span over that time was 20 years.

Even after the beginning of the common era, there have been times when populations suddenly declined in particular regions. In Europe, for example, where the population grew noticeably starting around the year 1000, it fell by one-third over just 60 years from 1340 to 1400 as a result of the plague known as the "black death." One out of every three people died. Regardless, the world population continued growing at an annual rate of approximately 0.06 percent, reaching 750 million around the middle of the eighteenth century at the dawn of the Industrial Revolution.

It was the Industrial Revolution that constituted a major turning point. The center of industry shifted from agriculture to manufacturing; as a result, there was continuous economic growth such as humanity had never before experienced. Per capita income rose rapidly, and along with that the population increased so quickly as to merit the term "population explosion." The annual population growth rate shot up to 0.6 percent, an increase of ten times the prior rate. The world's population increased tenfold over the next 200 years.

In the year 2000, the last year of the twentieth century, the world population surpassed 6.3 billion. What is more, it is expected to reach 8 billion in the year 2025 and 10 billion by the end of the twenty-first century.

According to biologists, the appropriate density for "large omnivorous animals" with a body weight of around 60 kilograms is 1.5 per square kilometer. The population density of humans living a hunting life that is nearly natural in Africa and other areas today is reportedly around three people per square kilometer. The worldwide average population density is now forty-four people per square kilometer, which is some thirty times the "appropriate density"; thus, the human population is clearly excessive (Hasegawa 2015).

Population decline is a big problem in Japan, but worldwide, population growth is still a problem. One could say that population decline is not a global problem, but one of certain countries, including Japan.

The problem of excess population

Looking back over the long history of humanity, some eras have seen sudden increases in population; conversely, there have been periods when populations have declined. Amid these fluctuations, "overpopulation" has been a major social problem when the population is too large in a given area, even though population decline like that seen in Japan today is sometimes also viewed as a problem.

Excess population was frequently an issue in ancient traditional societies where income levels were not sufficient to maintain people's lifestyles. Works by the ancient Greek philosophers Plato and Aristotle already included arguments on the need to limit population. In Japan, the stories of abandoning old women to die in remote locations—an extreme means of reducing the number of mouths to feed—are widely known.

In the Meiji period, the Japanese government began encouraging emigration to foreign countries as one means of resolving the overpopulation problem. In 1940, just before the start of the Pacific War, there were 760,000 Japanese living abroad (according to Ministry of Foreign Affairs, "1940 Statistical Survey on Japanese Nationals Overseas" in Kenji Kimura, *Kindai Nihonjin no kaigai imin* [Modern Japanese emigration], table 1). "Japanese nationals overseas" includes those living overseas for a short period of a few years, but it does not include those naturalized after emigration, so it does not accurately correspond to the number of emigrants. Nevertheless, it does indicate the approximate number.

In 1930, the literary giant Kan Kikuchi, who founded the publishing company Bungeishunjū, wrote about that era when a stifling feeling of entrapment increased day by day.

> While there may be causes such as difficulty finding employment and difficulty making a living, ultimately I think this is because there are too many people... There is no better idea to ease job shortages and hardships in life than reducing the number of people. Why don't we enforce restrictions on childbirth? It is really odd that such an obvious approach is not implemented immediately. If some assistant official with foresight in Tokyo City happened to begin a childbirth restriction project, a suspicious doctor of medicine would come running out from the Home Ministry and interfere. I do not understand why people in power do not implement childbirth restrictions even though the large number of people is believed to be destroying the nation.
>
> ("Konogoro no kansō" [Reflections on present times] in *Kaizō*, July 1930 edition)

In an address in May 1931, just before the Mukden Incident, Colonel Seishirō Itagaki—a staff officer in the Kwantung Army who was also the ringleader of the incident—made an appeal regarding the need for Japan to advance into Manchuria, citing the population problem as one reason:

> Compared to the population growth of 60,000 each year in our imperial nation with a small land area and scant resources, only 20,000 migrants are being sent overseas.
>
> (Kajima Institute of International Peace [ed.], *Nihon gaikōshi 18: Manshū jihen* [Japanese diplomatic history 18: The Mukden Incident]; Kajima Institute Publishing Company)

This perception was carried forward after the war. In *Nihon keizai zusetsu* (The Japanese economy illustrated), which was written by the Marxist economists Hyōe Ōuchi, Hiromi Arisawa, Yoshitarō Wakimura, and Ryōkichi Minobe in 1955, at the dawn of Japan's high-growth period, the authors noted that Japan has the third-highest population density in the world, and that "the ability of the national land area to sustain its population is extremely fragile." They concluded:

> Based on the above, it may be said that our nation's employment conditions have already reached their limits. Consequently, to provide employment for the working population, which continues to grow, the current scale of industry must be further expanded. If that is not realized, an increase in the number of unemployed will be unavoidable. The problem of overpopulation has only become more serious since the war.

Japan is by no means the only country to have promoted overseas migration to resolve its excess population. The migration of people from Ireland, Italy, Germany, and other European countries to the "New World" of the U.S. in the nineteenth and twentieth centuries is well known. The movie *Titanic*, for example, depicts such migrants and their feelings of anxiety and hope as they cross the ocean to the U.S. in a third-class cabin at the bottom of the ship.

Robert Malthus (1766–1834)

In this way, even many developed nations were troubled by overpopulation until the first half of the twentieth century. There were, of course, exceptions. In 1870–71, the "smallness" of the population was deemed a serious problem in France when it was defeated in the Franco-Prussian War against its neighbor Germany.

Well, then, how have economists viewed population issues? Before considering that topic, let us first examine the population increase in Europe from the eighteenth to the nineteenth centuries that provided the opportunity for the emergence of Robert Malthus, the author of *An Essay on the Principle of Population*.

The "population explosion" in modern Europe

What were the conditions of the population in West that opened the Pandora's box of modern economic growth through the Industrial Revolution? In 1750, the population of Europe—France, Germany, Britain, and other Western European countries, along with Sweden and other Northern European countries—was between 60 million and 64 million. Compared with the Chinese population of 300 million in the fifty-seventh year of the reign of Emperor Qianlong (1792), this was relatively small. However, the population of Europe increased to 116 million by 1850, basically doubling over 100 years. With an average annual growth rate of 0.7 percent, that can truly be called a population explosion.

The European population had previously increased at this rapid pace from the twelfth to the thirteenth centuries and also from the second half of the fifteenth century through the sixteenth century. But those population increases were halted by famine and communicable diseases in the fourteenth and seventeenth centuries, respectively, causing the population to revert to prior levels. In contrast, the population boom from the second half of the eighteenth century was distinguished by the fact that, despite the Irish famine in the 1840s, there was no decline in the population of Europe overall. Detailed research regarding the population increase in this period has accumulated in the relatively new academic field of historical demography. What follows is a summary of those findings (Anderson 1988).

As noted above, the population of Europe doubled from 60 million to 116 million over the 100 years from 1750 to 1850. This was attributable to changes in birthrates and mortality rates, but conditions varied substantially by country. While the mortality rates continued to decline in every country over those 100 years, there were great differences in the birthrates from country to country. In Britain, the birthrate rose from 3.4 percent in 1750 to 4.0 percent in 1820. In historical demography, the birthrate is often expressed as the number of children born per 1,000 people, but in this book this rate is expressed in percentages; that is, as the number of children born per 100 people, which is the ratio commonly used in economics. These are both "birthrates per unit of population" including men and children. We must note that they differ from the total fertility rate, which is the average number of children born per woman throughout her lifetime—a measure commonly used in Japan today.

In England, the increase in the birthrate was the cause of the population growth. This contrasts with the situation in France. Around 1750, the birthrate in France was 4 percent, which was the highest in all of Europe. That declined to 2.5 percent, the lowest level in all of Europe, 100 years later. Over that period, France experienced a revolution that was followed by the Napoleonic Wars, during which many young men died. In France, therefore, the decline in the birthrate cancelled out the decline in the mortality rate and the population hardly increased at all. Meanwhile, in Sweden and other Northern European countries the birthrates remained basically unchanged, but the populations increased due to the declines in the mortality rates.

In this way, the overall increase in the population of Europe from the eighteenth century through the first half of the nineteenth century had different underlying conditions in each country. After all, demographic trends are a complex phenomenon that cannot be explained simply.

Economists' view of population

The matter of population has drawn people's interest since ancient times, and of course many scholars have discussed it. As eighteenth-century Europe was undergoing a population explosion, it was only natural that the economists, who were pursuing an emerging academic discipline, discussed population amid the great changes in the economy caused by the Industrial Revolution.

Leaving aside the details of the debate, the standard way of thinking at the time was that a large population symbolizes social affluence while, conversely, a small population symbolizes poverty. In his 1776 book *Wealth of Nations*, Adam Smith (1723–90), who is known as the "father of economics," wrote, "The most decisive mark of the prosperity of any country is the increase of the number of its inhabitants" (book I, chapter VIII, "On the Wages of Labor"). Note that Smith does not say "the number" of inhabitants, but rather "the increase of the number." Here, Smith is also arguing that it is not the size of GDP (gross domestic product), but rather its continual increase that causes a rise in (real) wages.

Smith was not the only one who believed an increasing population was positive. Joseph Schumpeter (1883–1950), the author of numerous works on the history of economics, wrote that, through the middle of the eighteenth century, all economists were proponents of population growth.

> With rare exceptions, they were enthusiastic about "populousness" and rapid increase in numbers. In fact, until the middle of the eighteenth century, they were as nearly unanimous in this "populationist" attitude as they have

ever been in anything. A numerous and increasing population was the most important symptom of wealth; it was the chief cause of wealth; it was wealth itself—the greatest asset for any nation to have.

(*History of Economic Analysis*, chapter 5)

An Essay on the Principle of Population by Robert Malthus

It was Robert Malthus who then caused a sensation in the population debate. There is no book that has had a greater impact on future generations than *An Essay on the Principle of Population* (first edition, 1798) by Malthus, who lived during the period of great population growth in Europe. Most readers will surely have heard of this book.

Robert Malthus (1766–1834) was born in Surrey, England, in 1766, the second son of a wealthy farm proprietor who was friends with Jean-Jacques Rousseau and David Hume. He studied at Jesus College at the University of Cambridge, became a fellow of the college after graduation, and then became a curate in his home town. When the first edition of *An Essay on the Principle of Population* was published anonymously two years later, Malthus was only thirty-two years old and still a bachelor. While pursuing numerous debates with his contemporary, the famous economist David Ricardo (1772–1823), Malthus subsequently wrote several other works, including *Principles of Political Economy* and *The Measure of Value*, but he must have viewed *An Essay on the Principle of Population*, which he had written when he was still young, as his representative work. He devoted himself to revising this book over a period of nearly thirty years until the publication of the sixth edition when he was sixty years old. Unfortunately for Malthus, John Maynard Keynes (1883–1946) made the following comments about *An Essay on the Principle of Population* in his biography of his teacher, Alfred Marshall.

John Maynard Keynes (1883–1946)

> An Economic Treatise may have great educational value. Perhaps we require one treatise, as a *pièce de résistance*, for each generation. But in view of the transitory character of economic facts, and the bareness of economic principles in isolation, does not the progress and the daily usefulness of economic science require that pioneers and innovators should eschew the Treatise and prefer the pamphlet or the monograph?... Malthus spoilt the Essay on Population when, after the first edition, he converted it into a Treatise. Ricardo's greatest works were written as ephemeral pamphlets... Economists must leave to Adam Smith alone the glory of the Quarto, must pluck the day, fling pamphlets into the wind, write always *sub specie temporis*, and achieve immortality by accident, if at all.
>
> (Keynes, *Alfred Marshall, 1842–1924*)

The first edition of *An Essay on the Principle of Population*, which Keynes assessed as the most spirited, was a controversial book clearly aimed at a specific target. This book was written as a direct criticism of the amendment to the Poor Laws that was being advanced by the British government at that time. It was also a complete repudiation of the progressive view of history represented by William Godwin of Britain and Nicolas de Condorcet, who was active in France after the Revolution. Malthus' criticisms were based on none other than the famous "principle of population," which he himself established.

The principle of population

The Poor Laws, which were continued from the time of Henry VIII, Elizabeth I, and the other sixteenth-century monarchs of the House of Tudor, were a system similar to Japan's public assistance in which the state provided relief to the poor using taxes as the revenue source. At the end of the eighteenth century, when Malthus was alive, the British government implemented a reform to raise the level of benefits provided to the poor. Malthus was vehemently opposed to such government reform.

Being a curate, Malthus cannot have been indifferent to the plight of the poor, but the criticism he voiced was entirely logical. The point of his criticism was the population. In discussing population, the young Malthus began from two major principles: "First, that food is necessary for the existence of man. Secondly, that the passion between the sexes is necessary and will remain nearly in its present state" (Malthus, *An Essay on the Principle of Population*).

Malthus declares that these two truisms are "fixed laws of our nature" that cannot be changed. He writes that, as a consequence, population will increase where there is food; this, however, leads to the harsh reality that "population, when unchecked, increases in a geometrical ratio" while food "increases only in an arithmetical ratio." Malthus explains this using the following numbers.

> Assume the world population is 1 billion. While the population will increase at the rate of 1, 2, 4, 8, 16, 32, 64, 128, 256, 512, etc., food will only increase at the rate of 1, 2, 3, 4, 5, 6, 7, 8, 9, 10, etc.

This is the proposition that everyone immediately thinks of when speaking about Malthus' *An Essay on the Principle of Population*.

Malthus' argument that population increases in geometric progression when sufficient food is available was not without basis. He focused on the U.S. as an example of a country with conditions that are advantageous for population growth. The British colony declared itself independent as the United States of America in 1776, when Malthus was ten years old. In the northern states known as New England, the population roughly doubled every twenty-five years. On this basis, Malthus explained that even if the population and the food supply were initially in balance, they would eventually diverge. As an example, he stated that in 225 years the ratio of the population to the food supply would be 512 to 10, but in 300 years it would expand to 4,096 to 13.

Quantitative methods

The year 1798, when Malthus first published *An Essay on the Principle of Population*, was the tenth year of the Kansei era, marking nearly 200 years of the Edo period in Japan. Many books concerning economics and politics were published in Japan by Confucian scholars. However, unlike the fields of Japanese mathematics and astronomy, almost none of the discussions regarding society and the economy in Japan were supported by numerical evidence. These discourses remained entirely speculative.

In England, on the contrary, from as early as the late seventeenth century, William Petty (1623–87) argued in *Political Arithmetick* (1690) that, like studies of phenomena in nature, examinations of events in human society require quantitative analysis. Petty, who was a medical doctor, was a man of many talents; along with Isaac Newton and others, he helped found the Royal Society. In that era, quantification was not limited to physics but had become a key word for human affairs. This was a key difference between Japan (Asia) and Europe at the time.

Regarding the method and stance of his argument, Petty writes:

> The Method I take to do this, is not yet very usual; for instead of using only comparative and superlative Words, and intellectual Arguments, I have taken the course (as a Specimen of the Political Arithmetick I have long aimed at) to express my self in Terms of Number, Weight or Measure; to use only Arguments of Sense, and to consider only such Causes, as have visible Foundations in Nature;

> leaving those that depend on the mutable Minds, Opinions, Appetites, and Passions of particular Men, to the Consideration of others.
>
> (Petty, *Political Arithmetick*)

Malthus' inquiries clearly adopted Petty's mentality. Based on the figures derived from the population growth in the U.S. and other countries, and the reality of British agriculture, Malthus was convinced that population would increase in a geometrical progression, barring some constraint ultimately based on food supply.

But how do constraints on population actually work? Malthus believed population is constrained by people's fears that they will not be able to raise a child even if they have one, and by their consequent delaying of marriage or choosing not to marry. Such constraints should take effect in the poorer classes of society. After noting that many male and female servants were in fact unmarried, Malthus wrote that one could determine whether a nation's population is increasing or decreasing by dividing the number of unmarried individuals by the entire population to determine the percentage of unmarried people. He also made a point of cautiously noting that this percentage is related to increases or decreases in population, and not to the size of the population—that is, the population level.

From here, Malthus began his criticism of the reform of the Poor Laws. The idea behind reforming the Poor Laws and increasing the level of benefits provided was, of course, to raise the standard of living of people suffering from poverty. However, Malthus stated that even if increasing the level of benefits raised the standard of living of poor people temporarily—and even more so if the effect were large—in the end this would only increase the population and thus, the lives of the poor would inevitably return to their prior wretched conditions and remain unchanged. According to Malthus, as long as the total food supply remains the same, redistributing income to the poor cannot result in improvement of their living conditions over the long term. Continuing with his harsh argument, he wrote that if the number of people who marry but cannot provide for their families increases and the population expands, ultimately the population will inevitably be reduced by famine and disease. He says that compared with such misery, it is better for the population to be restricted in advance by poor people realizing the difficulty of supporting a family and therefore giving up on marriage.

Malthus simply summarizes the logic that supports his argument once again around the middle of *An Essay on the Principle of Population* (at the end of chapter VII) as follows: "That the increase of population is necessarily limited by the means of subsistence. That population does invariably increase when the means of subsistence increase. And that the superior power of population is repressed, and the actual population kept equal to the means of subsistence, by misery and vice." This argument by Malthus was subsequently denounced by Karl Marx (1818–83).

Dispute concerning the terms of trade

Malthus is an economist who, together with Adam Smith and David Ricardo, represents classical economics. For population to increase, the total food supply must increase. What is required for the food supply to increase? The vision of the young Malthus, including wages and prices, is presented in *An Essay on the Principle of Population*. Regardless, as Keynes noted, the attraction of the first edition of *An Essay on the Principle of Population* is above all its sharpness as a written argument, and not its being "economics written by a young economist."

While I will not enter into the economics of *An Essay on the Principle of Population* here, I do want to touch on just one point. The idea that the food supply does not catch up with population growth is a fundamental thesis of *An Essay on the Principle of Population*. Now, most of the population that increased in England was earning a living in the manufacturing sector, which was newly created by the Industrial Revolution. The growth of agricultural production is sluggish, as Malthus stressed using the example of arithmetic progression, but in manufacturing, high-paced growth is possible. What if England sold the goods it produced by manufacturing—an area in which it excelled—to the New World, where land was abundant, and then imported food from the New World? Would that not free England from the restrictions of its limited land area and support a larger population using imported agricultural products?

David Ricardo, who spoke against Malthus' views throughout his life, expounded on the benefits of free trade for England. Ricardo argued that England should specialize in manufacturing, in which it was internationally competitive, export manufactured goods, and import agricultural products from overseas. From this standpoint, he advocated the elimination of the high tariffs being imposed on wheat and other agricultural products.

In contrast, Malthus stressed that domestic agriculture should be protected by tariffs no matter what. He believed that the export of manufactured goods and the import of agricultural products would "temporarily" result in an increase in the amount of food consumed domestically, but that, even in the New World with its abundant land, the productivity of agriculture would gradually decline as new land was cleared. This was in contrast with manufacturing, where productivity does not decline much even when scale is expanded. As a result, he argued, the prices of agricultural goods would rise compared with the prices of manufactured products. In general, the prices of goods and services produced by low productivity sectors are higher than the prices of goods produced by high productivity sectors. Observe, for example, that while the prices of many home appliances are declining, the prices of services such as those at the barber shop are rising relative to the average price.

Malthus thought that if England exported manufactured goods while importing agricultural products, this would gradually lead to unfavorable terms of trade due to the rise in the prices of agricultural products. Here, the "terms of trade" is a conversion ratio that expresses the quantity of import goods a country can obtain in exchange for exporting one unit of export goods to a foreign country. Specifically, this is the export-goods-to-import-goods price ratio, calculated by dividing the export goods price by the import goods price. In the case of England, the terms of trade are the price of manufactured products divided by the price of agricultural goods.

Malthus believed that these would become disadvantageous for England over the long term, and that, consequently, importing agricultural goods could not be a fundamental means of resolving the population problem. In passing, a worsening of the terms of trade is one of the causes of the long-term stagnation of the Japanese economy in the twenty-first century.

Does human society progress?

In the latter half of *An Essay on the Principle of Population*, the focus of the argument shifts from the Poor Laws to the "progressive view of history" and the concept of an "equal society" as ideals espoused by William Godwin and the Marquis de Condorcet.

The English Godwin and the French Condorcet vociferously asserted the idea that human society is something that progresses. Malthus, who believed that human history—which may be said to be a struggle between population and food—is filled with misery and vice, and certainly does not progress, rejected this progressive view of history held by Godwin and Condorcet.

Condorcet, who wrote *Sketch for a Historical Picture of the Progress of the Human Mind*, lost his life in the chaos following the French Revolution. Malthus maintained a cold-hearted viewpoint toward this ardent supporter of the French Revolution, which advocated liberty, equality, and fraternity. In his *Essay on the Principle of Population*, Malthus sharply criticized Condorcet:

> To see the human mind in one of the most enlightened nations of the world, and after a lapse of some thousand years, debased by such a fermentation of disgusting passions of fear, cruelty, malice, revenge, ambition, madness, and folly as would have disgraced the most savage nation in the most barbarous age must have been such a tremendous shock to his ideas of the necessary and inevitable progress of the human mind that nothing but the firmest conviction of the truth of his principles, in spite of all appearances, could have withstood.

To begin with, Malthus describes the French Revolution itself as the "height of folly." There are two ways of seeing this conflict. One is the positive viewpoint that it liberated mankind from the yoke of feudal oppression and opened the door to modern society. In Japan, this positive assessment of the French Revolution as a battle for liberty, equality, and fraternity, which should still be viewed as ideals by mankind today, is probably dominant.

In contrast, the British conservatives represented by Malthus and by Edmund Burke, who wrote *Reflections on the Revolution in France* (1790), denounce the French Revolution in no uncertain terms as the historical folly of humanity. They argue that, since there are limits to human reason, efforts to construct an ideal society led by reason will inevitably fail. They hold that what should be the linchpin of society is wisdom that has been filtered in the long flow of history; that is, "tradition."

In *An Essay on the Principle of Population*, what Malthus attacks is the "equal society" that Condorcet and Godwin see as ideal. Malthus states that inequality is inevitable under the "natural law" of conflict between population and food.

> It has appeared, that from the inevitable laws of our nature, some human beings must suffer from want. These are the unhappy persons who, in the great lottery of life, have drawn a blank. The number of these claimants would soon exceed the ability of the surplus produce to supply.

Such indifference! Malthus then states further,

> The substitution of benevolence for self-love as the moving principle of society, instead of producing the happy effects that might be expected from so fair a name, would cause the same pressure of want to be felt by the whole of society, which is now felt only by a part. It is to the established administration of property and to the apparently narrow principle of self-love that we are indebted for all the noblest exertions of human genius, all the finer and more delicate emotions of the soul, for everything, indeed, that distinguishes the civilized from the savage state; and no sufficient change has as yet taken place in the nature of civilized man to enable us to say that he either is, or will ever be, in a state when he may safely throw down the ladder by which he has risen to this eminence.

According to Malthus, if population and food had increased at the same pace and there was no poverty, then humanity would surely have indulged in idleness and never emerged from the savage state. He says that humans made efforts and advanced civilization precisely because of the pressure of poverty.

Malthus referred to the imbalance between population and food and to poverty as a mechanism that limits population as "natural laws." When reading *An Essay on the Principle of Population*, even though this is a book about human society, one gets the feeling that Malthus views human society as if he were observing some insect world. In fact, it was Charles Darwin (1809–82) who was greatly impressed by this book and went on to write his immortal work on the evolution of plants and animals. In the introduction to his *On the Origin of Species* (1859), Darwin acknowledges Malthus as follows:

> In the next chapter [chapter III] the struggle for existence amongst all organic beings throughout the world, which inevitably follows from their high geometrical powers of increase, will be treated of. This is the doctrine of Malthus, applied to the whole animal and vegetable kingdoms. As many more individuals of each species are born than can possibly survive; and as, consequently, there is a frequently recurring struggle for existence.

Darwin gained the inspiration for his well-known theory of "natural selection" from Malthus' *An Essay on the Principle of Population*.

Keynes' *Economic Consequences of the Peace*

When speaking of British economists who were active in the first half of the twentieth century, some 100 years after

Malthus, John Maynard Keynes comes to mind. From his youth, Keynes felt an attachment to Malthus, who also graduated from the University of Cambridge, and he wrote a biography of Malthus. While this is not very well known, Keynes also had a strong interest in population.

Keynes worked for several years in the India Office after graduating from university, but he grew tired of the life of a civil servant, returned to Cambridge, and began teaching economics in 1908. As a young instructor, Keynes gave a lecture entitled "Population" in May 1914, just before the outbreak of World War I. The draft of this lecture (not included in his *Collected Writings*), which had long been sleeping at the bottom of the University of Cambridge archives, was discovered at the end of the twentieth century (Toye 2000).

Keynes' brilliance had been recognized by those around him since his youth, but his bestseller *The Economic Consequences of the Peace* (1919) made his name renowned worldwide. A peace conference was held in Paris at the end of World War I, and Keynes accompanied the British government delegation. The Treaty of Versailles concluded there strongly reflected the intentions of France, which was one of the victors and also the host country. The treaty demanded harsh reparations payments from the defeated Germany. Keynes perceived this treaty as nothing more than unrealistic vengeance that made no contribution whatsoever to the stability and peace of Europe, and he resigned from the British diplomatic corps after voicing his objections. Immediately afterward, he penned his worldwide best seller *The Economic Consequences of the Peace*, which has been translated into thirteen languages, including Japanese.

Right at the beginning of that book, Keynes shows his awareness that the Great War marked the end of an era. This perception was shared by contemporary European intellectuals who had the ability to foresee the future, and it was proven to be correct in light of the subsequent history. Keynes wrote that, even amid this extreme chaos, France, Germany, Italy, Austria, the Netherlands, Russia, Romania, and Poland were all part of a single world which shared a common civilization as Europe. He acknowledged that Europe was facing a crisis—one that was being made worse by a man-made disaster: namely, the Treaty of Versailles.

Keynes' argument began from an analysis of Europe before the war. He argued that, in retrospect, the seemingly unshakable prosperity of Europe over the fifty years following the late nineteenth century was built on an unstable economy, like a castle built on sand. Starting in the 1870s, along with the growth of the population of Europe, migration to the New World also increased; the supply of agricultural goods grew rapidly as the New World was developed; and, until around the start of the new century in 1900, the price of agricultural goods kept falling relative to the price of manufactured products. The terms of trade had changed in a direction that was favorable for Europe, which exported manufactured products and imported agricultural goods. In this way, good fortune—what Malthus would have laughed off as an "El Dorado" that was not realistically possible—continued for some decades in Europe in the latter half of the nineteenth century.

This good fortune brought Europe prosperity. In June 1914, however, it was destroyed by the shot that assassinated Archduke Ferdinand, setting the war in motion. The pressure of population increase that Malthus had warned of, which had been held in check during those decades of prosperity, finally came to a head.

After this introduction, Keynes analyzed the current conditions; the first theme he raised was none other than population. He drew attention to how the population of Germany, which was 40 million in 1870, rapidly expanded to 68 million in 1914. Keynes attributed this population increase to Germany's transformation from a largely self-sufficient agricultural country into a powerful industrial nation, and blamed this population increase for bringing about the expansionism of Germany which led the world into war.

The favorable terms of trade that created prosperity in Europe had already been worsening from the beginning of the twentieth century, before World War I. The age of El Dorado had already become a thing of the past by the time the war broke out.

In the prosperous nineteenth century, the inequality of wealth brought about economic development through savings. The nineteenth century conservatives argued that if the wealth/income created by a single country were equally divided among its people, it would all be consumed by the people, so savings would not occur among society as a whole. They held that, because inequality exists, the wealthy, who have surplus funds, use them for savings, which become the accumulated capital that advances the economy. In other words, inequality was a "necessary evil" for the progress of human society. This was the line of thought of the nineteenth-century conservatives.

According to Keynes, however, that social order was

destroyed by World War I. Savings could no longer be expected to have the positive effect of advancing the economic system. Savings that are not linked to investment are simply not consumed, and create insufficient demand in the economy. At this point, inequality is no longer the origin of economic growth, but instead becomes a constraint.

The devastation of the Great War was added at this major historical turning point. Even though Europe was facing a major crisis, the Treaty of Versailles demanded harsh reparations payments from Germany based on a childish desire for revenge. This delayed the postwar reconstruction and was creating a new crisis. *The Economic Consequences of the Peace*, which was filled with ideals and historical vision, brilliantly weaving in a levelheaded analysis of the conditions of that time, brought the young Keynes lasting fame.

"Some Economic Consequences of a Declining Population"

In 1937, eighteen years after he wrote *The Economic Consequences of the Peace*, Keynes presented a lecture at a Malthus-related population research center. This was the year after Keynes published his main work, his *General Theory of Employment, Interest and Money* (1936), which perfected what came to be known as Keynesian economics. The lecture was entitled "Some Economic Consequences of a Declining Population."

In contrast to Malthus' era, when writers never stopped expounding the evils of population growth, the problem facing Britain in Keynes' heyday, during the 1920s and 1930s, was the impact on the economy from population decline. This was not limited to Britain. In France, which had been defeated in the Franco-Prussian War (1870–71), there were already warnings of a crisis at the end of the nineteenth century, as France's population began to decline in comparison to that of its neighbor Germany, which was growing. The times had changed: population decline had already become a major problem.

Keynes pointed out that England had reached a major turning point, going from an era of population growth to an era of population decline; he said that the future would be a completely different world from the past. Above all, Keynes emphasized the influence of population on investment. Unlike the situation when Malthus and Ricardo were writing about economics, manufacturing had already become the leading industry. Manufacturing requires large-scale capital stock, such as factories and machines that are in an entirely different dimension from the plows and hoes used for agriculture. What increases capital is the capital investment each year. This is easily understood by comparing it to the water in a swimming pool. The amount of water in the pool at any given time is the "stock," which corresponds to capital. The amount of water that flows into and out of the pool each minute is the "flow," which corresponds to the investment year by year.

The total amount produced by a country's economy in a given year (that is, its gross domestic product, or GDP) is the flow. This consists of our consumption, along with private investments, as well as exports, public investments, and other government expenditures. Unless something extraordinary happens, consumption does not change drastically, as becomes clear from looking at our lives as consumers. In contrast, corporate investment is an "unruly horse." The increase and decrease in this investment generate the business cycles that accompany a capitalist economy. This is what Keynes argued in his *General Theory*, published in 1936. Therefore, when considering the long-term change from a growing population to a shrinking population, Keynes first examined the effect on investment.

What factors determine investment over the long term? Population is certainly one, as it determines the scale of the economy. Nevertheless, it is, of course, not the only factor. Technological advances, which boost our standard of living, also have a large effect on investment. The durability of capital is another important factor that determines investment. This third concept of the durability of capital is a bit difficult to understand. The easiest way to explain the term as used here is to present a few examples. While they both constitute housing, solid apartments built from stone are obviously capital stock with higher durability than the tents used by wandering nomads. Compared with automobiles, bicycles are capital with low durability. In other words, even for capital that provides the same type of service or production capacity, that which is larger and sturdier is the capital with higher durability.

According to Keynes, when we look over history from that perspective, large and highly durable objects were characteristic of Victorian civilization in the nineteenth century. This is exactly the impression we get when seeing the grand stone buildings on the streets of London. The civilization of the twentieth century, compared to the Victorian era, is an era of lighter capital goods. This point made by Keynes is naturally convincing today, when highly convenient goods are best characterized as being small and lightweight.

Capital stock that is highly durable and large naturally requires a sizable investment. But a small investment is sufficient for small, lightweight capital. If we can no longer expect highly durable, large capital stock, then population growth and technological advances that raise the standard of living are the only factors remaining to generate investment. However, we cannot expect enough technological advances to boost investment sufficiently. Moreover, the population is declining. With this reasoning, Keynes warned that, if left unchecked, the growth of investment in Britain after World War I would inevitably lack vigor.

If investment, which may be called the engine of capitalism, is insufficient, the economy falls into a recession. This is the conclusion of the *General Theory*, which was published in 1936. There may be people who want to work, along with sufficient machinery and factories to produce goods, yet plants and equipment stand idle and unemployment occurs. This is because the goods cannot be sold even if they are produced: the demand is insufficient. Such a recession may be characterized as "poverty in the midst of plenty."

The Devil P, the Devil U

The academic forerunner to the "macroeconomics of insufficient demand" stressed by Keynes was actually Malthus. Contrary to Ricardo, Malthus defended the land-owning class. In response to criticism that the extravagant consumption by the land-owning class was simply wasteful spending, like hunting, which gives no benefit at all to society, Malthus stated that what seems at first glance to be wasteful consumption by the land-owning class generates employment.

Keynes named the vice and misery brought forth by excessive population, as explained by the young Malthus, "the Devil P" (for "population"). On the other hand, he called the unemployment problem that Malthus noted when he was older "the Devil U" (for "unemployment"). The Devil P had made itself felt throughout the long history of mankind through to the first half of the nineteenth century. But in the twentieth century, with a declining population, Britain was exposed to the Devil U as a result of insufficient investment.

According to the French historian Jean Delumeau, fear is always present in human society. In the past, natural disasters, epidemics, and other nonhuman phenomena were the greatest threats to humanity. But since the twentieth century, two world wars have taken place, and nuclear weapons and also terrorism have become causes of fear. In addition, the threat of economic difficulty, such as unemployment or poverty, is great. In a survey conducted in 2014, more than 50 percent of those polled in seven leading EU countries responded, "In the future, the children's generation will be worse off financially than their parents'" (Global Attitudes Survey, spring 2014). Also, in Japan, in an opinion poll conducted in 2016 by NHK on youth aged eighteen and nineteen, who had newly gained the right to vote, 38.4 percent responded "I think Japan's future is bright," but 60.9 percent responded "I do not think Japan's future is bright." There is great anxiety about the future worldwide. The Devil U that Keynes identified in the 1930s certainly still roams the world today in the twenty-first century.

Under a declining population, what is required to keep the Devil U at bay and enjoy abundance? Keynes argued that consumption must increase to compensate for insufficient investment. In the nineteenth century, when there were any number of investment opportunities, savings were linked directly to investment, and therefore savings by the rich contributed to the progress of the economic system through capital accumulation. But that era ended. Keynes said that robust investment cannot be expected in the twentieth century, and that consumption has to uphold effective demand in place of investment. To those ends, there has to be income redistribution from the wealthy who save their income to the general public who consume. This essentially sums up what Keynes said in his lecture in 1930s Britain, a nation which had entered a period of population decline.

In Sweden

We have reviewed how Malthus and Keynes, two leading economists in Britain—which was the front-runner in global economics for 200 years, from the eighteenth century through the first half of the twentieth century—thought about population. We cannot forget about Sweden, another country that, along with England, made a great contribution to the discussion of population.

Today, Sweden is known worldwide as a welfare state, but it did not achieve that status overnight. In Sweden, the population debate was led by many economists in whom the country takes pride. Knut Wicksell (1851–1926) was a great economist who was active from the late nineteenth century through the early twentieth century. Wicksell is well known as a theoretical economist, but he originally gained interest in economics from his concern about the population problem. He was also a radical social activist who advocated for his own theories on population .

Wicksell's highly renowned *Lectures on Political Economy* (in Swedish; 1901) began with a chapter titled "Population Theory, Population Composition, and Population Change," but this chapter was removed from the second edition, published in 1910. Wicksell was incarcerated in 1909 for radical speech and behavior, and during his two months in jail he published this chapter on the population problem as a separate pamphlet.

Wicksell's reasoning regarding population was superb, as one would expect, and his careful analysis of population statistics has not lost its freshness even today. One distinctive point of his argument is his assertion that every country has an "optimum population." Leaving aside population increases and decreases, what would an "optimum population" be to begin with? The maximum population that a country can support was discussed as a standard for arguments about excessive population in the past, but an "optimum population" is a different matter. According to Wicksell, an "optimum population" is the population level at which any further growth would cause the average level of social welfare to decline. In other words, the "optimum population" is one that maximizes the average level of social welfare per capita.

Organizing his argument in this way, Wicksell concluded that the populations of the countries of Europe had greatly surpassed their optimum levels. Accordingly, he held that the correct policy would be to cause a population decline over some decades. Restrictions on childbirth are an effective method, but they contravene traditional religious views; it was on this point that Wicksell's words and actions caused friction with society.

Wicksell made an interesting point, however. He characterized as alarmist the oft-raised concerns that if efforts are made to intentionally reduce population, that could become difficult to stop, ultimately leading to the annihilation of society. With this concern, if a desire to increase the population emerged, he said, financial assistance given to families with many children should cause the birthrate to rise immediately. Wicksell was surprisingly optimistic about the effectiveness of subsidies to raise birthrates. His emphasis on reducing populations that are larger than their optimum size was a belief he never renounced, even when he was imprisoned for it.

The origin of childcare support

Wicksell struggled alone with the population problem. Gunnar Myrdal (1898–1987; 1974 Nobel Prize in economics) inherited Wicksell's spirit, and he succeeded in exerting a great influence on actual policy from a different standpoint. *Crisis in the Population Question*, which Myrdal wrote together with his wife Alva, drew a reaction in Sweden and had a strong influence on the policies of the Social Democratic

Party, which had long been in power. The article "Population Problems and Policies," which he wrote while living in the U.S., succinctly summarizes the Myrdals' viewpoint.

In the twentieth century, the trend of population reduction became clear to everyone, but many people were welcoming this as a "rise in per capita income" or even as freedom from the shackles of the "surplus population" that had plagued humanity throughout our long history, that is, as a symbol of the progress of civilization. Against this, the Myrdals made a strong case that not addressing population decline is an error.

Since per capita income admittedly rises when one has fewer children, this makes a single individual or family that much wealthier. However, the consequent reduction in the population of the country overall "is absolutely detrimental to the standard of the whole people." The Myrdals wrote that the benefits to individuals from restrictions on childbirth and the benefits to society overall are not the same.

The Myrdals did not insist on prohibiting birth control from a conservative viewpoint. They wrote that birth should be an individual's choice and that the right to birth control based on individual choice must be respected. On the other hand, just as support for the elderly was converted from allowances from within the household to the use of public pensions as a system for all of society, they argued for a system in which the burden of birth and child rearing would be shifted from individual households to society as a whole.

> The burdens [of child support] must be borne by the citizens as taxpayers, regardless of their having children

> or not. . . . The general method of population policy may therefore be described as the transfer of income from individuals and families without children to families with children.
>
> (Gunnar Myrdal, *Population Problems and Policies*)

This is nothing but what we call "childcare support policies" today. We are impressed that the Myrdals preferred subsidies in kind over cash benefits. Specifically, they proposed such policies as increasing the number of childcare facilities and improving levels of hygiene and education.

Policies to increase population were implemented by Nazi Germany and fascist Italy in the 1930s, but the Myrdals stressed that the population policies they themselves were proposing were completely different from the policies of such countries. While Germany and Italy aimed to promote childbirth, "[w]e only wanted to remove the hindrances preventing ordinary persons from following the natural urge to get married and have children" (Myrdal, 1938). This, of course, is the basis for the childcare support policies of the industrialized nations in the twenty-first century. The Myrdals proposed a new population policy to Sweden—an industrialized nation which was facing a declining population during the 1930s, seventy years before Japan was grappling with this issue—and had a large impact on actual policy formation.

Looking back over the long history of humanity, it becomes clear that the debate regarding population has run in every possible direction. Even now, the overall population of Earth is excessive. Within industrialized nations, however, the trend toward population decline is ongoing, and the shift to an aged society with a declining birthrate is creating a variety of social problems.

Population decline is unquestionably a major issue here in Japan. In the next chapter, let us first consider specifically what types of problems are generated by a declining population in social security, public finance, and regional communities.

While population decline is a big problem, excessive "population decline pessimism" is also spreading regarding the growth of the Japanese economy. Many argue there will be no future for the Japanese economy as the population declines. This is wrong, however, because economic growth in industrialized nations is fundamentally sparked by innovation, not by the working-age population. This is explained in detail in the next chapter.

Population Decline and the Japanese Economy

The administration of Shinzō Abe, which was formed in December 2012, attracted attention domestically and globally by advocating the "Abenomics" economic policy which comprised the "three arrows" growth strategy of aggressive monetary easing under a zero interest rate, flexible fiscal expenditure, and structural reforms. In October 2015, three years after Abe took office, as part of the "Abenomics" second stage, the government made population an important policy by announcing the goal of "putting a brake on the shift to an aging society with a low birthrate and maintaining a population of 100 million even fifty years from now."

As stated at the beginning of chapter 1, according to the "Population Projection for Japan" (medium fertility assumption) released by Japan's National Institute of Population and Social Security Research, Japan's population will decline to 50.50 million in the year 2115. This means the population, which is presently 127 million, will decline to less than half its current level over the next 100 years. We will reach an era of sudden population decline that is more rapid than the population declines Keynes and Myrdal were addressing as problems in Britain and Sweden during the 1920s and 1930s. The aging of society will also rapidly advance during this period. In response, the Japanese government has announced a policy goal of maintaining a population of 100 million in 2065, by which time the population will have declined to 81 million if no action is taken.

Will Japan disappear?

Population decline with a low birthrate and the rapid aging of society present grave problems for Japan's economy and society. This is really beyond a serious issue; if the population continues to decline in this way, the nation of Japan will disappear.

The number of children fourteen years old and younger in Japan, which was over 16.32 million on April 1, 2014, declined to 16.17 million on April 1, 2015, dropping by 153,000 in a single year. That number fell further to 16.05 million in May 2016, posting a decline for the thirty-fifth consecutive year since 1982. According to the *Nihon no kodomo jinkō dokei* (Web clock for counting the number of children in Japan) on the website of the Research Center for an Aging Economy and Society at the Tohoku University Graduate School of Economics and Management (Professor Hiroshi Yoshida; https://sites.google.com/view/caestop/JCCC), if the number of children in Japan continues to decline at this pace, it will be reduced to one on August 14, 3776. That would make for a very sad Children's Day ! There are still 642,870 days remaining until that time (as of July 1, 2016).

It goes without saying that such a dramatic decline in population is itself a major issue. Even if it does not reach the point of Japan actually disappearing, the aging of society alongside the declining birthrate is already creating severe problems. One of these is social security and the burden on public finances; another is the impact on regional communities.

Social security for a super-aged society

Along with population decline, the aging of society has also been advancing at a remarkable speed (chart 2-1). Japan became an "aging society" in 1970, when the percentage of

Chart 2-1. Advance of an Aging Society with a Low Birthrate

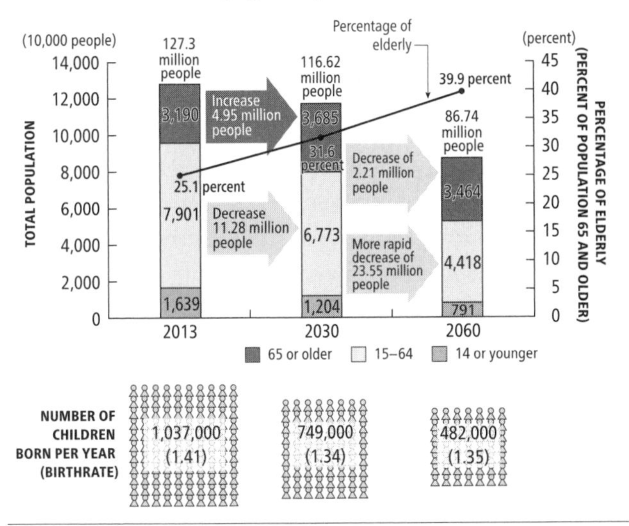

Sources: Ministry of Internal Affairs and Communications, *Population Census of Japan*; National Institute of Population and Social Security Research, "The Three Fertility Variants with Medium-Mortality Assumption" (population as of Oct. 1 each year), *Population Projections for Japan (January 2012)*; Ministry of Health, Labour and Welfare, *Vital Statistics*.

Note: Totals do not match because of rounding (the same hereafter).

the elderly (people sixty-five or older) in the total population exceeded 7 percent, and became an "aged society" in 1994 when the ratio exceeded 14 percent, and then finally became the world's first "super-aged society" when the ratio exceeded 21 percent in 2007. According to the 2015 census, 26.7 percent of the Japanese population are elderly. The ratio of the working-age generation (between fifteen and sixty-four) to the elderly, which was 11 to 1 during the high-growth era, had already fallen from 2.5 to 1 in 2013; it will drop from 1.8 to 1 in 2030, and then from 1.3 to 1 in 2060, when the percentage of Japanese who are elderly is projected to peak.

Such a high proportion of elderly people creates major problems for society and the economy. As everyone knows, the economic power and health of the elderly varies greatly. Most company presidents and directors are sixty-five or older. On the other hand, there are elderly who have no income sources aside from pensions. While some older people are blessed with good health, many suffer from grave illnesses and require nursing care. This is nothing new. Mencius, a Chinese philosopher from the fourth century B.C., wrote:

> There were the old and wifeless, or widowers; the old and husbandless, or widows; the old and childless, or solitaries; the young and fatherless, or orphans—these four classes are the most destitute of the people, and have none to whom they can tell their wants...

Mencius concluded that the government must support people who are in such positions of weakness. Unfortunately, a complete resolution to the problems faced by socially vulnerable people is difficult, but at least a system to mitigate this situation exists, and that is none other than the social security system.

Today, Japanese social security "benefits" (money and services provided to those who qualify) total ¥116 trillion per year. Japan's GDP is ¥500 trillion, so this is a huge figure approaching one-fourth of GDP. The unit "trillion" is a massive number beyond our practical experience. It would take a stack of ¥10,000 bills 10 kilometers high to reach ¥1 trillion. The Japanese economy is generally discussed in terms of trillions of yen.

Pensions of ¥56.2 trillion (FY 2015) account for roughly half the total benefits, followed by ¥37.5 trillion for medical care, ¥9.7 trillion for nursing, and ¥5.5 trillion for "children and childcare." Social security benefits also include unemployment insurance, which pays unemployment benefits when people are out of work, and public assistance, which is called the "final safety net" (see chart 2-2, upper half).

When money or even services are provided, the costs must be borne by someone in some manner. With respect to the social security burden, 60 percent is covered by insurance premiums, half of which are paid by labor and half by management, while the remaining 40 percent is paid for by taxes (chart 2-2, bottom half). Even though we use the term "taxes" here, at present these costs are not directly paid using tax revenues; rather, they are covered by the issuance of deficit-covering bonds. So strictly speaking, we should really say "public expenditures" rather than taxes. As explained later on, this is the fiscal deficit problem.

Anyway, the ratio of 60 percent insurance premiums to 40

Chart 2-2. Current Status of Social Security Benefits and Obligations (based on FY 2015 budget basis)

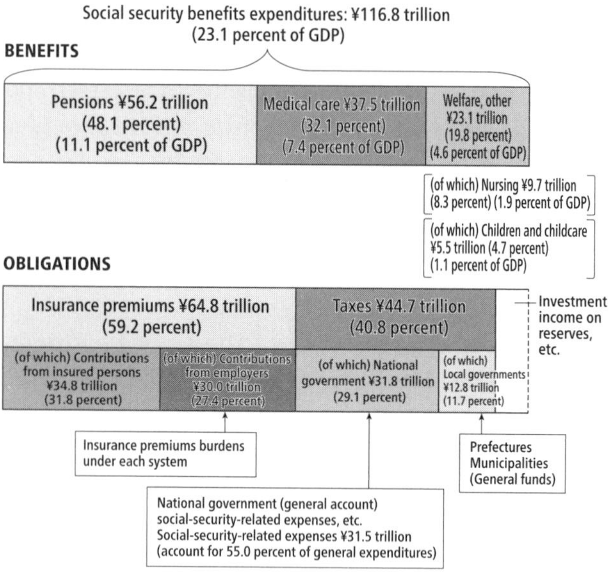

Social security benefits expenditures: ¥116.8 trillion
(23.1 percent of GDP)

BENEFITS

Pensions ¥56.2 trillion (48.1 percent) (11.1 percent of GDP)

Medical care ¥37.5 trillion (32.1 percent) (7.4 percent of GDP)

Welfare, other ¥23.1 trillion (19.8 percent) (4.6 percent of GDP)

(of which) Nursing ¥9.7 trillion (8.3 percent) (1.9 percent of GDP)

(of which) Children and childcare ¥5.5 trillion (4.7 percent) (1.1 percent of GDP)

OBLIGATIONS

Insurance premiums ¥64.8 trillion (59.2 percent)

Taxes ¥44.7 trillion (40.8 percent)

Investment income on reserves, etc.

(of which) Contributions from insured persons ¥34.8 trillion (31.8 percent)

(of which) Contributions from employers ¥30.0 trillion (27.4 percent)

(of which) National government ¥31.8 trillion (29.1 percent)

(of which) Local governments ¥12.8 trillion (11.7 percent)

Insurance premiums burdens under each system

National government (general account) social-security-related expenses, etc.
Social-security-related expenses ¥31.5 trillion
(account for 55.0 percent of general expenditures)

Prefectures
Municipalities
(General funds)

Note: Social security benefits funding sources also include investment income, etc.

percent taxes is for social security as a whole, but the shares of insurance premiums and taxes (national and regional) are different for each system. On the one hand, public assistance and the welfare systems for children and individuals with disabilities are covered completely by taxes, with no insurance premiums; on the other, no taxes are allocated for employees' pensions or health insurance (society-managed health insurance), which are covered entirely by insurance premiums. The burdens of the basic pension, national health insurance, latter-stage elderly healthcare system (for people

75 and older), and nursing care insurance are each covered half by taxes and half by insurance premiums. In this way, the systems are varied and complex. These current conditions were not designed based on any clear policy—they are the products of compromises reached in the past.

The insurance premiums, which account for 60 percent of the burden, are paid by businesses together with the working-age generation, and income taxes and other taxes are also paid by the working-age generation. So, social security costs are mostly borne by the working-age generation. As for the benefits, the elderly receive pensions, and they are also the primary recipients of medical care and nursing care. Incidentally, while the average annual medical expenses per person are ¥175,000 for people aged sixty-four and younger, this figure rises to ¥553,000 for those sixty-five to seventy-four, and to ¥892,000 for those seventy-five and older. Thus, the per capita medical expenses for later-stage elderly people aged seventy-five and older are more than five times those for the working-age generation (Ministry of Health, Labour and Welfare, "FY2011 Overview of National Medical Care Expenditures").

If the low birthrate causes the working-age generation to shrink and the aging of society causes the number of elderly people to increase, social security benefits will consequently balloon, while the revenues that support them will taper off. Financing social security becomes increasingly difficult for an aging society with a low birthrate. The national budget must then be geared to rescuing social security from financial trouble, but that exacerbates the fiscal deficit, which is yet another problem for Japan.

The danger of financial collapse

Japan's fiscal deficit is a huge problem, as is widely known today. The outstanding stock of public debt attributable to the national government and local governments (prefectural and municipal governments) combined—that is, the total of Japanese public bonds—reached ¥985.2 trillion at the end of FY 2015, amounting to 195.1 percent of GDP.

Japanese government bonds are the debt of the national government, so some think they must be repaid down to the last penny, but repayment is already impossible. In fact, the outstanding balance of Japanese government bonds (excluding municipal bonds) was ¥838 trillion as of the end of FY 2016. Dividing that by the total population of 126.19 million, from newborn babies to centenarians, Japan's national debt is ¥6.64 million per person. Anyone would sigh thinking of how much this is for a four-person household.

But there is a misunderstanding here. Even though Japanese government bonds represent the national debt, there is no need for the outstanding balance to be repaid to the last yen and reduced to zero. Or, more precisely, if the balance of Japanese government bonds were reduced to zero, the conduct of monetary policy itself would no longer be possible. Not only for the "aggressive monetary easing" that began in April 2013, but in general, the monetary base is supplied in part by the central bank purchasing Japanese government bonds from private banks. Circumstances under which the balance of Japanese government bonds would become zero are actually not desirable.

Then what is the problem with the fiscal deficit? It is this: the balance of Japanese government debt, which keeps growing as a result of the fiscal deficits each year, has become too large. It is like the water that collects in a ship's bilge. If too much water collects in the bilge, the ship will sink like the *Titanic*. It cannot be said as a rule how many tons of water it takes to sink a ship, because the answer of course differs for a large ship such as the *Titanic* and a small fishing vessel. The danger level must be judged with a relative view of the amount of water in the bilge and the size of the ship. This also holds true for the level of government debt. The size of the economy—that is, GDP—corresponds to the size of the ship. Consequently, the ratio of the outstanding balance of government debt to GDP is used as a measurement to express the level of danger of fiscal bankruptcy, or, conversely, as an index to express the health of the nation's finances.

At or below what level can the outstanding government debt-to-GDP ratio be deemed to indicate sound government finances? While there is no definitive answer, EU member states are obliged to maintain a government debt-to-GDP ratio of 60 percent or less. In fact, while the fiscal balance of each country worsened (tax revenues slumped while expenditures increased) under the worldwide recession following the bankruptcy of Lehman Brothers in September 2008, in most industrialized nations the ratio of government debt-to-GDP remained below 100 percent. As seen above, in Japan the government debt-to-GDP ratio (strictly speaking, the ratio of public debt, including municipal bonds, to GDP) has already reached 200 percent, and it continues rising with no sign of slowing. This is Japan's fiscal deficit problem. If the current conditions persist, the nation's finances will eventually collapse.

However, some say the status of Japan's government finances is not as severe as the government debt-to-GDP ratio indicates and that such predictions of financial collapse are just confusing the public, often basing this on the following argument. While Japanese government bonds are the debt of the government, the government also holds assets along with its financial obligations. Looking at the net debt after deducting the assets from the debts, Japan's government finances are not as bad as they are said to be. However, many assets held by the government, such as pension deposits and government buildings, cannot be sold off to repay the debt. This argument that the conditions indicated by the net debt are not that bad is not convincing, given the current status of Japan's government finances.

There is also the argument that, while most of the national bonds of Greece, which defaulted, were held by foreigners, Japan is not at risk because Japanese government bonds are held by Japanese nationals (including the Bank of Japan and private-sector financial institutions). But no one would say that the share price of a private enterprise is dangerously high because the shareholders are foreigners or safe because they are Japanese nationals. Share prices are determined by a company's fundamentals, that is, by its management abilities, technological strengths, marketing, and so forth, regardless of the nationality of the shareholders. Ultimately, the fundamentals concerning government bonds are the soundness of government finances. So, the argument that Japan's finances are sound because the bondholders are Japanese nationals is also wrong. In short, Japanese government finances are in a severe condition, with a public debt-to-GDP ratio exceeding

200 percent, and will inevitably collapse if measures are not implemented.

Why do Japan's fiscal deficits continue expanding?

Why did Japan's public finances become so bad to begin with? The water in the bilge of the ship (stock) accumulates from the water that enters from holes in the ship each hour (flow). In the same way, the current outstanding balance of government bonds (stock) is none other than the accumulation of the annual fiscal deficits (flow) from past years.

Chart 2-3 presents the transition of Japan's fiscal balance (general account) over the past forty years. This shows that the fiscal deficit expanded from the collapse of the bubble

Chart 2-3. Transition of Government Expenditures and Revenues

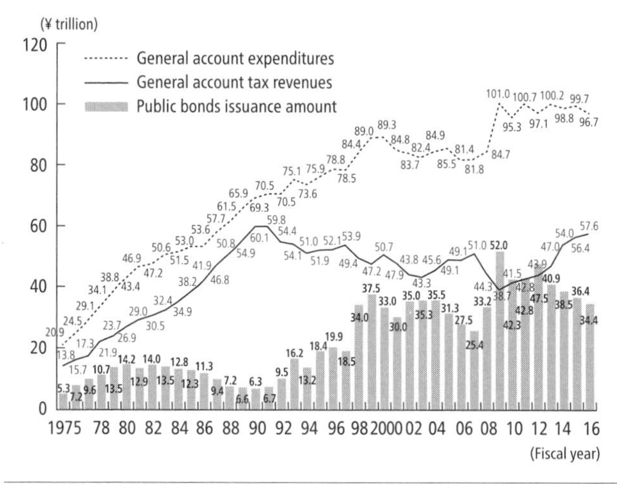

Source: Ministry of Finance.

economy at the start of the 1990s, just after the beginning of the Heisei era. The deficit shrinks when business conditions are favorable and expands during recessions. That is the truth, and in fact the fiscal deficit shown in chart 2-3 fluctuates from year to year. Nevertheless, looking at chart 2-3 overall, it becomes clear that Japan's fiscal deficit is a long-term problem that should certainly be called "structural." Obviously, it cannot be solved by economic growth alone. The fiscal deficit is simply the gap between expenditures (the amount of money spent from the budget) and revenues (the amount of taxes and other money that comes into the government). Fiscal deficits expand from an increase in expenditures, a decrease in revenues, or both.

Here, we focus on expenditures. Budgets reflect their times. The contents of expenditures change along with shifts in the economy and society. Chart 2-4 presents such changes in the shares of expenditures. Looking at the general account budget for FY 1960, a few years before the 1964 Tokyo Olympics, its scale was ¥1.7 trillion. This included ¥200 billion budgeted for social welfare, representing only two-thirds of the ¥300 billion budgeted for public works. During this period, the construction of roads and other infrastructure was urgent. This was a time when there were many dirt roads where puddles would form when it rained, even in Tokyo.

Thereafter, Japan's government budget continued to expand during the economic growth of the 1960s and also during the 1970s, despite the end of high growth and the oil crises, and it reached ¥69 trillion in FY 1990 just before the bubble economy collapsed. Japan then entered the 1990s, which have been called "the lost decade," and public works

Chart 2-4. Changes in General Account Main Expenditures

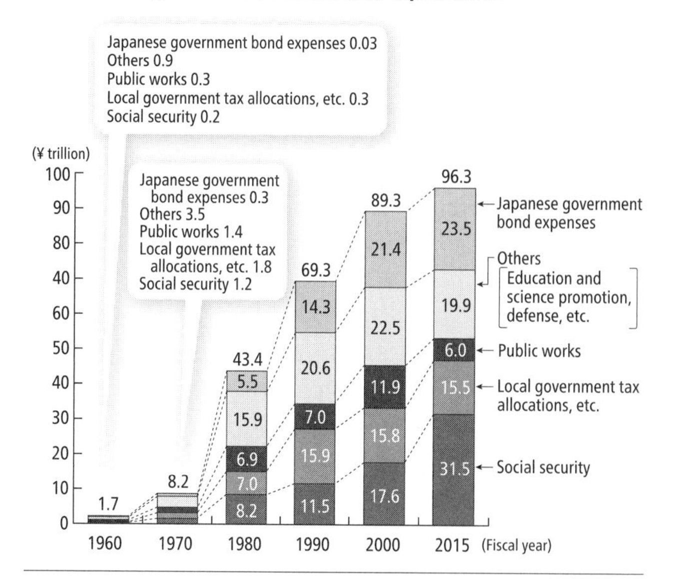

Source: Ministry of Finance.

expenditures expanded dramatically under a series of economic stimulus measures during the severe recession. Starting in the 2000s, however, public works expenditures were greatly cut by a series of governments starting with the Koizumi administration; they were decreased to ¥6 trillion, about half the FY 2000 level, in FY 2015.

Amid such changes in the times, there are two expenditures that have consistently increased since the 1970s. One is the debt-servicing expense on Japanese government bonds. When the balance of Japanese government bonds rises because of the cumulative government debt, the interest expenses increase along with the bond repayment expenses as a matter of course. But it is social-security-related expenses that have grown year by year by even more. Today, excluding debt servicing and tax allocations to local governments, which are transfers to municipal governments from the general account budget, over half of Japan's "policy expenses" are now social-security-related expenses (¥31.5 trillion / ¥57.4 trillion = 55 percent in FY 2015).

Social-security-related expenses constitute an overwhelmingly high share of the nation's budget, and with the aging of society, they are projected to increase by nearly ¥1 trillion each year. As explained above, as the working-age generation, which pays insurance premiums, shrinks due to the declining fertility rate, benefits will increase from the aging of society, so the social security reserves will become strained. Because this gap is covered by the social-security-related budgets of the national government and municipal governments, it is hard to prevent those budgets from ballooning due to the aging of society with a declining birthrate. Thus, the demographics have created the major problem of the fiscal deficit.

To resolve this problem, while restricting the growth of expenditures, increased revenues (that is, increased taxes) are clearly necessary. I will not delve into this any further here. But I will mention that we Japanese need to carefully consider the fact that the EU—which, like Japan, is struggling with the aging of society—has a rule imposing a minimum consumption tax (value-added tax) of 15 percent in member countries.

Will municipalities disappear?

There is another big problem caused by an aging society with a low birthrate and a declining population. In May 2014, the Depopulation Problem Subcommittee of the Japan Policy Council (chaired by Hiroya Masuda, former governor of Iwate Prefecture) issued a report entitled *Seichō o tsuzukeru 21 seiki no tame ni 'sutoppu shōshika': Chihō genki senryaku* (For a twenty-first century with continued growth, stop declining birthrates: Strategies for revitalizing non-metropolitan areas) (Masuda 2014). This report is a valuable information source with easily understood explanations about the impact on regional economies and other implications of population decline. It proposes advancing a comprehensive strategy based on the following types of basic policies to stop serious population decline and revitalize local regions.

First, the Japanese people do not fully understand the severity of population decline in Japan. This tends to be thought of as something in the distant future, but excessive optimism can be dangerous. So, awareness of the issue needs to be shared.

As a specific measure, considering that the actual fertility rate is lower than desired, efforts can be made to boost it by removing factors that discourage people from having children. To those ends, efforts are being made to create an environment where it is easy to get married, give birth, and raise children in one's twenties and early thirties, and where it is also easy to bear and raise a second and a third child.

One of the reasons "Stop Declining Birthrates: Strategies for Revitalizing Non-metropolitan Areas" was picked up by the mass media and became a topic of conversation was that it calculated its own estimates of the impact on population from future population dynamics at the municipal level. Population projections by region have also been prepared by the National Institute of Population and Social Security Research (March 2013). The difference between these two estimates lies in the assumptions made when considering the shifts in population among regions. When preparing estimates, the important point is the straightforward fact that women between the ages of twenty and thirty-nine give birth to most children. In 2012, when the total fertility rate was 1.41, some 95 percent of the births were by women in this age range. So, it is reasonable to focus on the population of women between the ages of twenty and thirty-nine when making future estimates.

Young women are still moving away from certain regions. Even if this were not a factor, with the present total fertility rate of 1.41, the number of young women will decline by 30 percent in thirty years. To maintain the population, the total fertility rate must immediately be increased to 2.00. The National Institute of Population and Social Security Research estimates assume that the outflow from these regions will decline to roughly half by 2020. However, if the percentage of young men and women who move outside these regions remains at around 30 percent as in the past, the number of young women will decline by half in thirty years, and it will become impossible to stop population decline even if the birthrate increases. It is quite possible, then, that such municipalities will disappear. This is the scenario assumed by the report.

The expression "disappear," which was used in the report,

had a large impact. According to an estimate by the National Institute of Population and Social Security Research, Japan has 373 municipalities (20.7 percent of the total) where the population of young women will decline by at least 50 percent through the year 2040, including 243 (13.5 percent) where the total population will be less than 10,000 in 2040. In contrast, under the estimate in the report, which assumes the same future population outflow as in the past, Japan will have 896 (49.8 percent of the total) municipalities where the population of young women will decline by at least 50 percent through the year 2040, including 523 (29.1 percent) where the total population will be less than 10,000 in 2040. Thus, there is a high likelihood that about 30 percent of Japan's municipalities could "disappear" over the next twenty-five years.

To be sure, this is not the first time that depopulation has been addressed as a serious problem in Japan. It was taken up as a major problem in the 1960s with the influx of population from agricultural villages to metropolitan areas.

However, the population decline and aging of society that are presently advancing are having an unprecedented impact on Japan's economy and society. One example is water supply, which is essential to our lives. Waterworks are operated by municipalities, but in places with considerable population decline the water rates have to be increased to maintain business operations. In Bibai City, Hokkaido, the rates were raised by 30 percent in October 2015 (*Asahi Shimbun*, September 7, 2015 morning edition). And the difference in rates among regions is consequently expanding. Monthly household water bills now vary by nearly ten times from a maximum of ¥3,510 in the town of Naganohara in Gunma

Prefecture to a minimum of ¥367 in Akō City in Hyōgo Prefecture (April 2014). What is more, in Kagawa Prefecture, where there is a fourfold differential within the prefecture, a plan is being advanced to integrate the waterworks of each municipality into a single entity.

In this way, population dynamics have a large effect on local regions. As seen above, along with the birthrate, one of the most important factors affecting local regions is interregional migration. Accordingly, for regional vitality, the government has put forth the policy goal "from the cities to the regions," which is the opposite direction of the population movement up until now. However, people who relocate do so of their own will, without being forced by anyone. How has the migration of population among regions changed historically? Let us now give some consideration to this issue.

Urban population rankings in the Meiji period

There is no doubt that the human species has been migratory since ancient times. Human beings originated in Africa, and dispersed throughout Eurasia and across the Bering Sea to the Americas. The reasons for migration certainly included scarcity of food, changes in the natural environment, and other factors that pushed people from their regions. Even without such negative changes in the environment, however, our ancient ancestors would suddenly climb over mountains, cross rivers, and migrate. When I once complained that I could never do any such thing, an anthropologist laughed at me, saying, "That is what humans do." We are animals, and I suppose that means we are animate beings.

Chart 2-5. Changes in Population of Japanese Cities

	1878		1920		1985	
	POPULATION (1,000 PERSONS)	RANK	POPULATION (1,000 PERSONS)	RANK	POPULATION (1,000 PERSONS)	RANK
Tokyo*	671.3	1	2173.2	1	8354.6	1
Osaka	291.6	2	1252.9	2	2636.2	3
Kyoto	232.7	3	591.3	4	1479.2	6
Nagoya*	113.6	4	430.0	5	2116.4	4
Kanazawa*	107.9	5	129.3	11	430.5	31
Hiroshima*	76.7	6	160.5	8	1044.1	10
Wakayama*	62.1	7	83.5	23	401.4	39
Yokohama	61.5	8	422.9	6	2992.9	2
Toyama*	58.4	9	61.8	35	314.1	55
Sendai*	55.0	10	119.0	12	700.3	12
Sakai	45.7	11	85.1	22	818.3	13
Fukuoka*	45.5	12	95.4	17	1160.4	8
Kumamoto*	44.6	13	70.4	27	555.7	16
Kobe	44.1	14	608.6	3	1410.8	7
Fukui*	41.6	15	56.6	37	250.3	80
Matsue*	36.5	16	37.5	63	140.0	140
Niigata	35.6	17	92.1	19	475.6	24
Tottori*	34.7	18	29.3	77	137.1	141
Hirosaki*	33.4	19	32.8	73	176.1	115
Okayama*	33.3	20	94.6	18	572.5	15
Nagasaki	32.6	21	176.5	7	449.4	26
Kagoshima*	32.1	22	103.2	14	530.5	17
Hakodate	31.2	23	144.7	9	319.2	58
Akita*	31.0	24	36.3	67	296.4	61
Takamatsu*	30.2	25	46.6	48	327.0	53
Morioka*	29.5	26	42.4	53	235.5	90
Kōchi*	29.1	27	49.3	44	312.2	57
Matsuyama*	28.1	28	51.3	41	426.7	28
Yonezawa*	27.7	29	43.0	52	93.7	218
Hikone*	27.5	30	17.7	–	94.2	212

Sources: Tominaga 1990. Figures for 1878 are from Sekiyama 1942. Kobe and Hyōgo are combined. Figures for 1920 and 1985 are from the census. In 1920, Hikone was not recognized as a city.

An asterisk (*) indicates a former castle town.

Leaving aside the Ice Age and other times in the ancient past, however, it is rare in modern and contemporary times for people to migrate impulsively. When many people do migrate, there are economic or social forces at work. In that regard, let us consider the shifts in population in Japan starting in the Meiji period, in the latter half of the nineteenth century. Chart 2-5 shows the changing population rankings of Japanese cities (Tominaga 1990).

In 1878, the Edo period was gradually becoming a thing of the past. Looking at the urban population rankings in chart 2-5, setting aside the largest cities from number 1 (Tokyo) to number 4 (Nagoya), the rankings from number 5 on down might surprise many people. Edo (the former name for Tokyo) previously had a population of a million people and was one of the largest cities in the world along with Naples, but its population dropped by half within just a few years amid the chaos of the Meiji Restoration. In 1878 the population of Tokyo was 670,000, yet that was the largest in Japan. The second-largest city, Osaka, was rather small compared with Tokyo, with 290,000 people. The third-largest, Kyoto, had 230,000, and the fourth-largest, Nagoya, had 110,000.

While those rankings are more or less as one would expect, surprisingly Kanazawa was the fifth-largest city, with almost 110,000. In 1878 the Kaga domain, which had an income of 1 million *koku* of rice, was still powerful (as ruling family of the Kaga domain, the Maeda's income of 1 million *koku* was one of the largest amongst feudal lords, second only to the Tokugawa shogunate's income of 8 million *koku*, in its peak in the middle of the 17th century). Other cities whose prominence may seem surprising include number 7,

Wakayama; number 9, Toyama; number 15, Fukui; number 16, Matsue; number 18, Tottori; number 19, Hirosaki; number 29, Yonezawa; and number 30, Hikone.

As shown in chart 2-5, the relative populations of these cities subsequently decreased, and their rankings declined. One noticeable fact is that these cities are in regions that face the Sea of Japan or are in the Tōhoku area of northeastern Honshu. These urban population rankings from 1878 may seem surprising to us today, but they are actually not so unnatural, because at that time the country's principal industry was agriculture, which had been continued from the Edo period. Because agriculture uses land, it gains no benefit from agglomeration; rather, it must be dispersed throughout the country. The cities with large populations in 1878 were the centers (former castle towns) of their respective regions; that is, the domains of the Edo period. Their economies were based on agriculture.

As shown by the chart, Japan's urban population greatly changed over the subsequent 100 years. The greatest reason for these shifts was that the foundation of industry switched from agriculture to manufacturing. Unlike agriculture, manufacturing benefits from agglomeration. The advancement of Japan's industrialization centered on the Pacific side of the country. As a result, many of the cities that had high population rankings from the Edo period through to 1868, when the Meiji period began, started to experience relative population declines.

The Japanese government is now advancing the policy of "from the cities to the regions." To be sure, there are problems with the unipolar concentration in Tokyo. However, there are limits to the migration of population by directions from on high; these must have some rational basis.

What determines economic growth is not population

Population decline has a large impact on government finances, social security, and the future of rural regions, as explained above. Population decline is a major issue for twenty-first century Japan, but what sort of influence does this have on the growth of the economy?

A population decline means that the number of workers will decline. Consequently, many believe the Japanese economy will have zero growth at best, and—in all likelihood—we must prepare for negative growth. A large number of people probably think that the era of a growing economy is over and the era of a shrinking economy has begun. Such comments are frequently heard; in fact, corporate CEOs say they do not want to invest in plant and equipment in a country whose population is in decline. As related in chapter 1, in the 1930s Keynes said one could not expect much more investment in a Britain where the population was declining. This issue has two aspects: supply and demand.

First, let us consider the supply side. If the number of workers declines, the quantity of goods produced should certainly also decline. This logic is easy to understand, and really cannot be denied. However, the logic of this argument actually makes a large jump. GDP expresses the total value (strictly speaking, "value added") of goods and services produced by a country in one year, but its growth is definitely not

Chart 2-6. Population and Economic Growth in Japan (1870–1994)

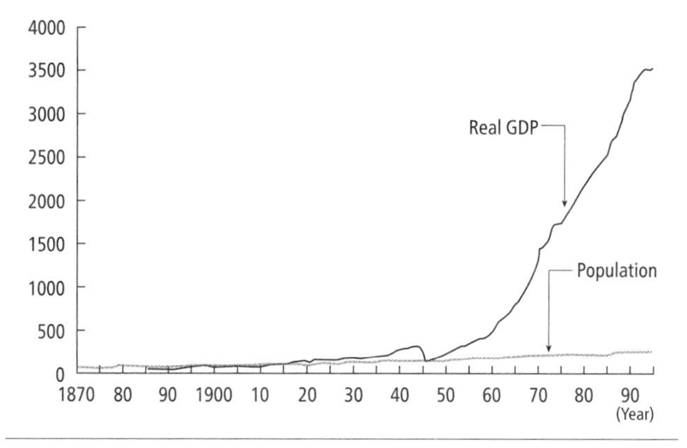

Source: Maddison 1995.

Note: Population and real GDP both indexed with 1913 = 100.

determined by the rate of increase in the number of workers (the labor force) alone.

To see is to believe. Chart 2-6 compares the shifts in Japan's population and real GDP over more than 100 years starting in 1870. The right half of the chart stands out because of the high postwar growth, but changing the focus and looking toward the left half only, one can see there was a large gap between GDP growth and population growth before World War II as well. These two are so separate that one could say that over the 150 years from the start of the Meiji period through to today, there is virtually no relation between economic growth and population!

The differential between the economic growth rate and the population growth rate is none other than the growth of labor productivity, which roughly corresponds to the growth of "per capita income." Even if the labor force does not change—even if it declines slightly—if the amount of goods produced by each worker increases (that is, if labor productivity rises), then economic growth will be positive.

The role of innovation

When we speak of labor productivity, some people associate this with workers' morale. While it is understandable to think that positive growth becomes possible if everyone works hard, that has its limits. I often hear it said that, in the end, if the labor force decreases, then zero growth is the best we can possibly expect. There are also people who think that labor productivity is the same as workers' physical strength and agility. From this they argue that because Japan's society is aging, labor productivity will not rise and is likely to decline. To be certain, elderly people do not have the physical strength and agility of people in their twenties and thirties. But the substance of labor productivity is not the morale or the physical strength of the workers. True, labor productivity does decline when there are major problems with people's health—in developing countries, for example—and when workers' morale sharply declines in countries with political instability or at companies where the relations between labor and management are poor. However, the opposite is not true. In the industrialized nations, including Japan, it is normally not workers' morale or physical strength that causes growth in labor productivity in the economy overall.

The biggest factors that cause increases in labor productivity in the economy of a country are capital accumulation—that is, investment in new facilities and machinery—and technological advancement in a broad sense—that is to say, innovation.

People who strongly connect the labor force with economic growth may have a picture of, say, road repair, where each worker has one shovel or pickaxe. Under this model, the output (products) inevitably declines when the number of workers shrinks. Economic growth in industrialized nations, however, is like a bulldozer appearing at a site where laborers had been working with shovels and pickaxes. In this way, labor productivity rises. In some cases, the work that was previously done by 100 people can now be accomplished by five. This is brought about by innovation and capital accumulation: the piece of equipment called the bulldozer was invented, and the construction company brought a bulldozer to the construction site for use.

The fact that such examples are not imaginary can be quickly understood by remembering the automatic ticket gates at train stations. Not long ago, up until the 1980s, ticket gates were manned by workers, even at Tokyo Station. Labor productivity shot up with the introduction of automatic ticket gates. For that to happen, of course, automatic ticket gates had to be invented, and the equipment had to be installed at train stations through the capital investment of the railway companies.

Soft technological advancement

At this point, it becomes necessary to add a little more explanation regarding innovation and technological advancement.

When technological advancement is mentioned, one tends to think of hard technology developed by scientists and engineers in scientific and technological fields. Of course, hard technology does play a major role in the technological advancement that contributes to economic growth. Its importance goes without saying. In economics, however, technological advancement is not limited to the progress of hard technologies. Along with them—and in some cases even beyond them—the "soft" technologies of know-how and management skills are important.

The coffee at Starbucks, which has taken the world by storm, does not in and of itself involve any particularly superior hard technologies. The key to this company's success lies in the comprehensive soft power of bringing a new concept, along with a manual and a brand, to the shop space that had been a tea house in Japan and a café in Europe. Because it created added value that is internationally competitive, the birth of Starbucks was truly a technological advance—an innovation.

Technological advancement in a country's economy as a whole—that is, in the macro-economy—is also brought forth by progress in the industrial structure. In 1950, for example, just before the high-growth era began, primary industries centered on agriculture accounted for one-fourth of the Japanese economy on a national income basis. Roughly half of all employed individuals were engaged in primary industries. At that time, the labor productivity in agriculture was around one-fifth that of modern manufacturing. Through the high-growth era, Japan's industrial structure underwent a great change: from agriculture to manufacturing, and then to tertiary industries. If labor and capital shift from low-productivity sectors to high-productivity sectors, then the labor productivity of the economy overall rises, even if the "hard" technologies in each sector remain unchanged—although of course, they did change as well.

The high economic growth era

Thus, macroeconomic labor productivity changes for various reasons. The issue becomes how large these changes are when viewed quantitatively. The best reference for this is past performance, but there are various ways of looking at performance. Here, let us consider the raw data focusing on the measurement of labor productivity.

Chart 2-7 compares two fifteen-year periods: one is the high-growth era (1955–70); the other is the era from the first oil crisis (1973–74) to the collapse of the bubble economy in

Chart 2-7. Relationship between Labor Force and Economic Growth

High-growth era

	1955	1970	AVERAGE ANNUAL GROWTH RATE
Real GDP	¥47.2 trillion	¥187.9 trillion	9.6%
Labor force	42.3 million	51.7 million	1.3%

From the first oil shock to the collapse of the "bubble economy"

	1975	1990	AVERAGE ANNUAL GROWTH RATE
Real GDP	¥234.2 trillion	¥463.1 trillion	4.6%
Labor force	53.44 million	64.14 million	1.2%

Sources: Real GDP: Cabinet Office, *National Accounts of Japan*. Labor force: Statistics Bureau, Ministry of Internal Affairs and Communications, *Labor Force Survey*.

1990. The chart shows the changes in real GDP and in the labor force (the combined number of persons employed and persons unemployed among the population who are fifteen or older). Japan's economic growth rate during the high-growth era was nearly 10 percent (9.6 percent in the chart). This was the period when the Olympics were first held in Tokyo (1964). Japan's growth rate declined to the 4 percent level during the period from after the oil crisis until the bubble economy collapsed.

Compared with the economic growth rate, the change in the labor force is relatively unknown. As shown in the table, the average annual growth rate in the labor force was 1.3 percent and 1.2 percent during the high-growth era and after the oil crisis, respectively: it hardly changed at all.

Just a quick glance at chart 2-7 indicates that Japan's high growth was not sparked by robust growth in the labor force. The high growth was caused by an increase in labor productivity (9.6 percent – 1.3 percent = 8.3 percent). Similarly, what cut the economic growth rate to 4.6 percent after the oil shock was not a decline in the labor force growth rate, but rather a decline of nearly 5 percentage points in labor productivity, which fell from 8.3 percent to 3.4 percent.

The mechanism of high growth

Economic growth is not solely determined by the growth of the labor force. It is necessary to think not only of the supply side of the economy but of the demand side as well. Economic growth, which is born under the alternate influences of supply and demand, is a complex phenomenon that may be called "historical." To understand this point, it is probably best to look at Japan's high-growth era of the fifteen years from around 1955 to 1970. While I would like to leave the details to my essay *Kōdo seichō: Nihon o kaeta 6,000 nichi* (High growth: 6,000 days that changed Japan), the high-growth mechanism can be summarized as shown in chart 2-8.

Japan in the 1950s, just before the high-growth era began, was a completely different world from today. In 1950, 48 percent of Japanese who were employed worked in primary industries such as farming, forestry, and fisheries; one out of every two working Japanese was a farmer. Many Japanese lived in three-generation households in agricultural villages. The houses in those villages, and even in the cities, had none of the things we take for granted today. They had no televisions; it was the age of radio. They had no electric washing machines; laundry was backbreaking work done by hand. They did have refrigerators, but these were cooled with ice rather than electricity, so the shopping districts of every city had ice stores where appropriately sized slabs of ice would be hewn from an ice block. There were no telephones. There were no fluorescent lights—only simple light bulbs. In short, houses, which were centered on tatami rooms, contained nothing beyond the bare necessities.

Japanese people came to desire the "three sacred treasures" of a black-and-white television, an electric refrigerator, and an electric washing machine, as well as other similar items. But at first, these were too expensive to be within reach of the common person. As shown in chart 2-8, a "virtuous cycle" eventually began, which was the high-growth era. It was manufacturing in the cities that led this change.

Chart 2-8. High Growth Mechanisms

(A) Domestic Cycle

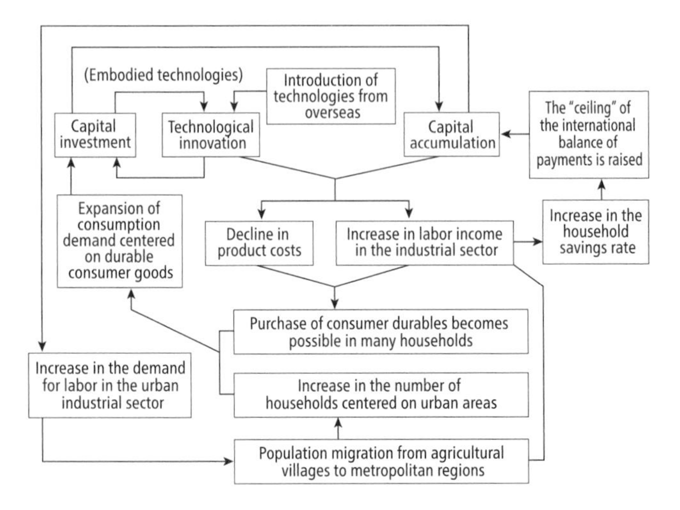

(B) Exports and Raw Materials Imports

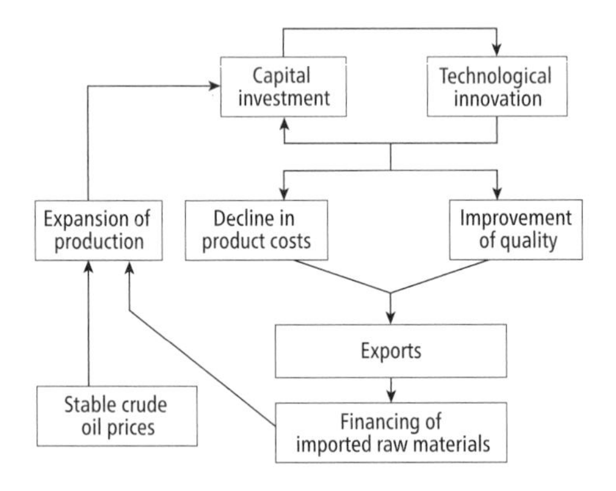

Source: Yoshikawa 2012.

Abundant technological innovation, along with investment in plants and equipment in the industrial sector, reduced the prices of goods that people wanted. For example, washing machines sold for ¥54,000 each when they were first released in 1949. This was roughly equal to the first-year annual salary of a public servant who had graduated from university, so it is no surprise that initially only twenty units were sold each month. But the prices dropped dramatically due to technological advancements and the mass production effect, and at the same time both productivity and the income of urban salaried employees rose. Over the six years from 1949 to 1955, the price of a washing machine fell by more than half to ¥20,000, while the average annual income of an urban salaried employee more than doubled from ¥140,000 to ¥360,000. In this way, by 1955, one out of every three Japanese homes had a washing machine.

With the development of manufacturing, the compensation of urban salaried employees rose sharply, and there was a labor shortage. Young men and women who in earlier times would have spent their entire lives in agricultural villages came to the cities in droves. The "group hiring" of fifteen-year-old boys and girls who had just graduated from junior high school was emblematic of the migration of people from rural villages to cities at this time.

People who moved to the cities formed new households. During the high-growth era, the number of households grew at a far higher rate than the actual population (chart 2-9). When a family is living in a three-generation household in a farming village, a single refrigerator and a single washing machine are enough, but when a young person forms a new

Chart 2-9. Number of Households and Population Growth Rates

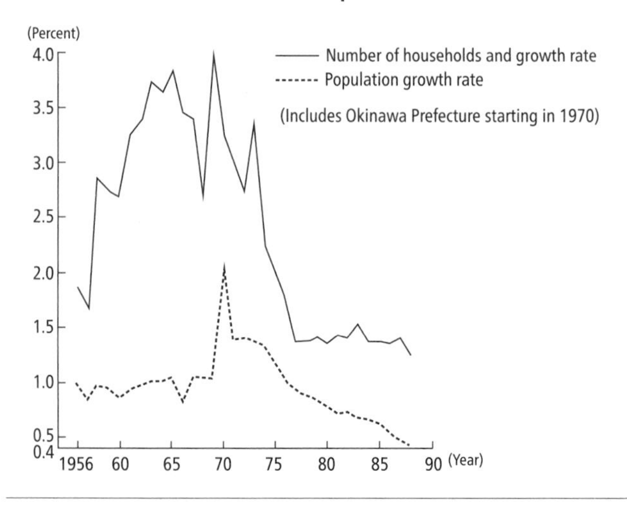

Source: Yoshikawa 2012.

household in the city, an additional refrigerator and washing machine are required. Of course, another house is required as well. Such changes were recognized by the policymakers while they were taking place. For example, the following point was noted at a roundtable held in 1967.

> MORITA: Now that the average [number of persons per household] is changing from five people to four people, even if the population does not increase, housing must be increased by 25 percent.
>
> UEDA: I noticed this the year before last. When they announced the approximate figures for the population and the number of households, I was surprised

that, while the population declined in twenty-five prefectures, the number of households did not decline in even one prefecture. I thought that this even by itself was a major change, and when I saw the results of the one percent sample tabulation, it became very clear.

("Shinshun zadankai: Jinkō kara mita Nihon no genjō to shōrai" [New Year's roundtable: Japan's present and future conditions from the viewpoint of population] in *Tōkei*, January 1967)

This increase in the number of households boosted domestic demand.

It is not well recognized even today that, during the high-growth era, the contribution to economic growth from net exports (that is, exports minus imports) was basically zero. Many have long believed that the growth in the Japanese economy was led mainly by exports, but that is absolutely not the case. The high growth averaging 10 percent per year was created not by exports but by robust domestic demand.

The spread of consumer durables that people desired, the migration of people from agricultural villages to cities, the consequent increase in the number of households—these were not "colorless and transparent" events that might occur in any age, but rather historical conditions that Japan's economy and society were subjected to only once, during the 1950s and the 1960s. High growth was born under such historical conditions. That economic growth is not a mechanical phenomenon dependent only on population increase should be clear from this review of Japan's high-growth period.

Will AI and IT steal people's jobs?

The fact that the economy can grow at a rate that far exceeds the population growth rate implies that changes in labor productivity (which can be restated as per capita GDP growth) influence economic growth more than changes in the labor force do. The economic growth of industrialized nations is created mostly by per capita GDP growth rather than population growth. As already explained, increases in labor productivity are not caused by the dedication, morale, or physical strength of workers, but rather by "technological advancement" in a broad sense; that is, by innovation, capital accumulation, changes in industrial structure, etc.

While some people are concerned about the decrease in the labor force, there are also warnings that the future demand for labor will fall due to newly created technologies, especially the development of information technology (IT) and artificial intelligence (AI). At its extreme, the fear is that people may be replaced by machines on the shop floor. The book *Race against the Machine*, by Erik Brynjolfsson and Andrew McAfee, is representative of this viewpoint.

The language comprehension abilities of AI are limited at present but steadily improving. The robot Tōrobo-kun, which is being developed at the National Institute of Informatics with the goal of having it pass the University of Tokyo's entrance examination, recently made news by scoring standard deviations of more than 60 for the first time, in mathematics and world history, in a mock National Center Test for University Admissions held in November 2015.

Will the jobs of human beings be replaced by Tōrobo-kun and other AI and IT entities someday? Several points require attention when considering this issue. First, are AI and IT replacing specific jobs that have been carried out by humans up until now, or are they replacing the work of all human beings? It is important to make a distinction between these two. If AI and IT are used to conduct certain types of work or operations that human beings have generally done in the past, this is something that has occurred repeatedly in history, and something we experience on a daily basis. The automated ticket gates mentioned earlier are a typical example. With the introduction of machinery, the demand for human labor—that is to say employment—is lost at certain job sites.

However, having automation take over a specific job at a specific workplace is completely different from wiping out the demand for all human labor. Many people easily fear that jobs will be lost as work long done by people is taken over by machines, perhaps because a specific image comes to mind. But looking back through history, the story is in fact the opposite. Wages rose because there was robust demand for labor in the economy overall, and a shortage of workers. In fact, it was rising wages that prompted firms to introduce machines for "labor saving" in certain operations. Originally, in eighteenth-century England, the steam engine was invented and improved by James Watt and others as a reaction to rising wages. AI and IT are different from those kinds of machines in that they replace the human brain. But how is this fundamentally different from the bulldozer, which took over work that previously had to rely on human muscle?

Another point that must not be forgotten is that it is humans who consume the goods and services produced by AI and IT, and to consume them, they must purchase them.

It obviously follows that the people who purchase goods and services must earn sufficient income to make such purchases possible. While I mentioned this already, looking back through history, much work that humans traditionally did has been taken over by machines. But humans were not "discarded" as a result. Rather, labor productivity rose and wages rose. In other words, humans became wealthy thanks to machines.

To explain this in somewhat greater detail, the income that humans earn while mechanization advances is the combination of the wages earned by labor and the income earned by ownership of the machines (the income gained from capital). So, in the AI and IT society, the income earned by people is the total of labor income and income gained from AI and IT property rights (including indirect interest income, etc.). Amid the advance of mechanization over the past 200 years of history, labor's share of income never crept downward. On the contrary, in industrialized nations, labor's share remained generally stable at a level of 60 to 70 percent. From this point onward, however, labor's share will continuously decline, while the share taken by capital will grow more and more, and the "society of great wealth inequality" will arrive—or so argues Thomas Piketty in his worldwide best seller *Capital in the Twenty-First Century*. At present, however, there are compelling theoretical and empirical arguments against Piketty's assertions.

Regardless of the past 200 years of history, is there really no reason to worry that AI and IT might render human labor completely unnecessary? This question was debated by the British economist David Ricardo, who was active more than

200 years ago, around the time of the Napoleonic Wars. Ricardo, who perfected the classical economics that began with Adam Smith, continued a debate for many years with Malthus, the author of *An Essay on the Principle of Population*. Ricardo's main work, *On the Principles of Political Economy and Taxation*, was published in 1817. Ricardo consistently maintained that the introduction of machinery advances the interests of workers. At the end of the third edition of *Principles*, published in his later years, however, Ricardo added a new chapter entitled "On Machinery" in which he conversely predicts that machines could be highly detrimental to workers' interests. The Swedish economist Wicksell, introduced in chapter 1, argued against this claim by Ricardo. This question was also subsequently addressed by Paul Samuelson, one of the leading economists of the twentieth century. (Incidentally, the title of his paper was "Ricardo was Right!" [Samuelson 1989]). Over the 200 years since Ricardo, so far, people have not been made poor by machines. Machines have always advanced the wealth of people in industrialized nations. But will AI and IT make Ricardo's prediction a reality in the twenty-first century?

The "Third Industrial Revolution" and Industry 4.0

Let us return to our main topic—the assertion that economic growth is impossible in Japan because population and the labor force are shrinking. The point of this chapter is that this argument is too simplistic. Also, regardless of whether or not it is true, the issue of AI and IT taking away people's work is completely contrary to fears that a decline in the population will mean that we cannot produce goods.

In relation to the fact that economic growth is not determined by the size of the population, there are other important points of debate. In 2012, the British magazine *The Economist* printed a feature article entitled "The Third Industrial Revolution." That article says that, while production work for the manufacturing industry of industrialized nations has been relocated to China and other Asian countries, the emergence of 3D printing and other developments have greatly reduced the amount of human labor required to produce goods. As an example, the article says that the manufacturing cost (raw materials and labor costs) of an Apple iPad with a retail price of $499 is $187, of which the labor cost in China accounts for just $8. The percentage of labor costs in production varies by industry. In any case, in the twenty-first century, the merit of being close to markets where new goods are sold will outweigh the merits of inexpensive labor. In this way, the production of goods will return to industrialized nations, according to *The Economist*.

Not long after this article in *The Economist* about a third industrial revolution appeared, the chancellor of Germany, Angela Merkel, personally took the lead in announcing "Industry 4.0," saying that a fourth industrial revolution has begun. Siemens and other top corporations have gathered at an artificial intelligence research center in southern Germany, where they are conducting tests to realize a "factory of the future," which will use AI and the Internet to optimally combine multiple production lines. This is also called IoT (the Internet of Things). The production of small volumes of a wide variety of goods without using manpower will be possible at this fully automated factory, which uses 3D printers controlled by AI and IT. This approach not only integrates the flow from the production of components through to sales of a single product; it aims at integration among industries. They say that, if this is realized, productivity in the German manufacturing industry will increase by 1.5 times within ten years.

It is still unknown whether the third and fourth industrial revolution will have as great an impact as the original Industrial Revolution in the eighteenth century did. In the meantime, changes that will be called a fifth and a sixth industrial revolution will certainly occur. While their trends are unknown, there is one thing we know for sure: the economic growth of industrialized nations is not determined by the number of people; rather, it is sparked by innovation.

The Fruit Called Longevity

As Keynes and Myrdal warned in the 1930s, the chief demographic challenge for industrialized countries in the twentieth century shifted from population growth to population decline. This population decline has begun amid prosperity.

To begin with, however, such population decline in wealthy industrialized nations runs counter to Malthus' principle of population, which holds that if the level of per capita income rises, then people will have lots of children and the population will increase. Even Darwin's *On the Origin of the Species*, which gained inspiration from Malthus, holds that various organisms compete with each other in gaining even a little more food in a struggle for existence, and those that succeed increase in number. In fact, in daily life today as well, we often hear explanations regarding increases and decreases in the populations of wild animals and birds based on this "principle," yet the number of humans has begun to decline at a time when per capita income is extremely high by any historical standard. That is not self-explanatory by any means.

Another thing that began in parallel with population decline was an increase in average life expectancy. Today, we view longer life expectancy as a matter of course, but this is also not ordinary by any means. Malthus strongly rejected the possibility that life expectancy would increase.

In this chapter, we once again consider the decrease in population and extension of life expectancy in the industrialized nations. As seen in the following chapter, these are also closely related to innovation.

The decline in birthrates in industrialized nations

Signs of population decline were already emerging at the end of the nineteenth century. Today hardly anyone recognizes the name of Lujo Brentano, one of the leaders of the once-thriving "German historical school." He was active along with Max Weber in Germany prior to World War I.

Brentano (1844–1931) investigated the demographic trends in Europe at the end of the nineteenth century and discovered that birthrates were declining even though average income levels were rising in every country. Based on this, he raised objections to Malthus' thesis. According to Malthus, when income levels rise, people should have many children and the population should grow, but Brentano discovered that the opposite was occurring. It is true that a country's overall birthrate is influenced by marriage rates, but he found that in fact it was a decline in the number of children per married couple that was having a large effect on the decline in the birthrate. Moreover, through a detailed examination of the birthrate in each country of Europe over roughly thirty years from the end of the nineteenth century through the beginning of the twentieth century, looking separately by region, income level, and occupation, Brentano found that while the birthrate was not declining in households with low incomes, it was falling noticeably among those with high incomes and educational levels. Brentano called this a "new reality" that cannot be explained by the principle of Malthus.

Why did the birthrate decline among wealthy people? Brentano addressed several points of debate from the prior research that are still being examined by experts today. Along with the progress of society, the variety of goods and services enjoyed by young people expands, and enjoying them takes more time and money. As a result, people avoid childbirth and childrearing, which require huge amounts of time and money. People have fewer children so they can maintain their high standards of living. They also want to give a small number of children access to higher education and allow them to enter professional occupations. In addition to such trends, changes in women's awareness have also been noted.

As one can easily imagine, it was wealthy people who were first affected by the changing times in which birthrates fell due to new entertainments such as going to the opera and traveling abroad, as well as changes in women's awareness and high educational levels. While the traditional birthrate was maintained among the middle- and lower-income segments, it was initially in the wealthy segment where the birthrate fell. When civilization prospers, contrary to what Malthus said, the population declines. Brentano's paper concludes by pointing out that the Roman Empire also declined in this manner.

To be certain, looking back over the long history of humanity, late nineteenth century Europe was not the first place where a wealthy nation experienced population decline.

For example, in "Girisha no suitai ni tsuite" (On the decline of Greece) in *Murakawa Kentarō kodaishi ronshū 1* (Collection of essays on ancient history by Kentarō Murakawa, vol. 1), professor of ancient Western history Kentarō Murakawa examines various theories regarding the decline of the city-state in ancient Greece and quotes Polybius, who was alive in the middle of the second century B.C. and wrote about Greece at that time.

> In our time all Greece was visited by a dearth of children and generally a decline in population, owing to which the cities were denuded of inhabitants, and a failure of productiveness resulted, though there were no long-continued wars or serious pestilences among us... For this evil grew upon us rapidly, and without attracting attention, by our men becoming perverted to a passion for show and money and the pleasures of an idle life, and accordingly either not marrying at all, or, if they did marry, refusing to rear the children that were born, or at most one or two out of a great number, for the sake of leaving them well off or bringing them up in extravagant luxury.
>
> (Polybius, *The Histories*, Book XXXVII:9)

As they say, history repeats itself.

Changes in Japan's birthrate

As Brentano discovered a century ago, the birthrate had begun to decline in the industrialized nations of Europe starting at the end of the nineteenth century, especially among the

Chart 3-1. Changes in the Number of Births and the Birthrate in Japan

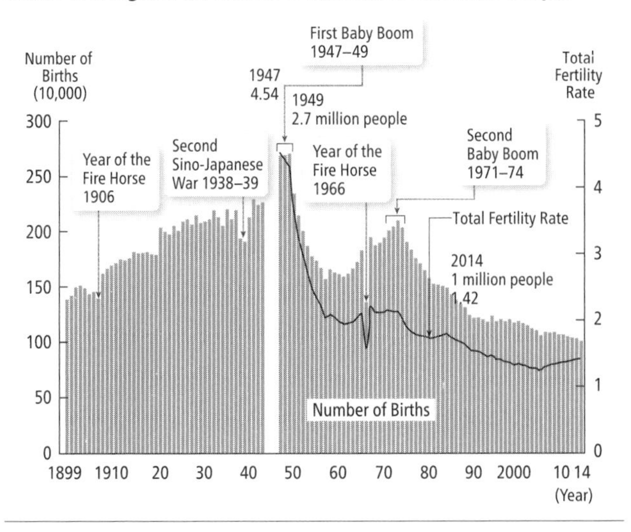

Source: Ministry of Health, Labour and Welfare, *Vital Statistics*.

economically wealthy class. Chart 3-1 shows the shifts in the number of births and the birthrate in Japan. To be precise, what is referred to as the "birthrate" here for simplification is actually the "total fertility rate." This is calculated each year by taking the numbers of children borne by mothers of each age between fifteen and forty-nine, dividing those by the female population for each age, and adding together the total. As mentioned in chapter 1, this is the average number of children a woman will give birth to during her lifetime.

In Japan, during the first half of the twentieth century before World War II, the birthrate rose overall, although there were effects from the Second Sino-Japanese War and the year of the fire horse 1906 (Japanese avoid giving birth in fire-horse years, as indicated by the Chinese zodiac, because women born in those years are considered too strong-willed to marry). After World War II, there was a noticeable jump in the birthrate, with the "baby-boom generation" born from 1947 to 1949. This was the peak of the twentieth century. An overall decline in the birthrate has generally continued since that time, although there was an increase in the number of children born from 1971 to 1974—the so-called second baby boom generation, who are the children of the first baby boomers.

Looking at the birthrates by the mother's age, as shown in chart 3-2, the decline among women in their twenties is conspicuous. Conversely, birthrates are increasing among women in their thirties, but this is because the marriage age has been rising as more couples delay marriage (chart 3-3).

Chart 3-2. Changes in Birthrates by Mother's Age

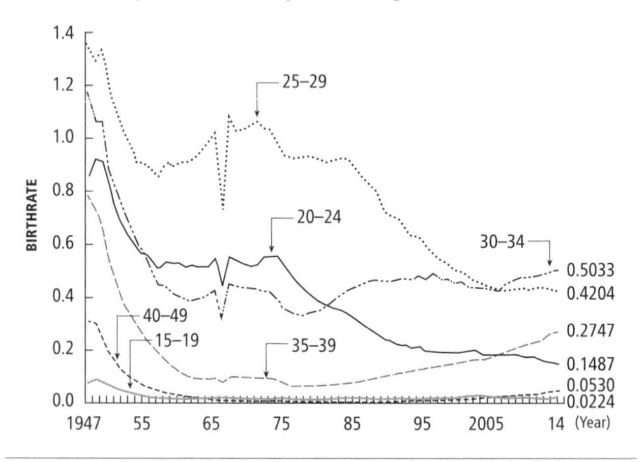

Source: Ministry of Health, Labour and Welfare, *Vital Statistics*.

Chart 3-3. Rise in Percentage of Unmarried Men and Women by Age Group

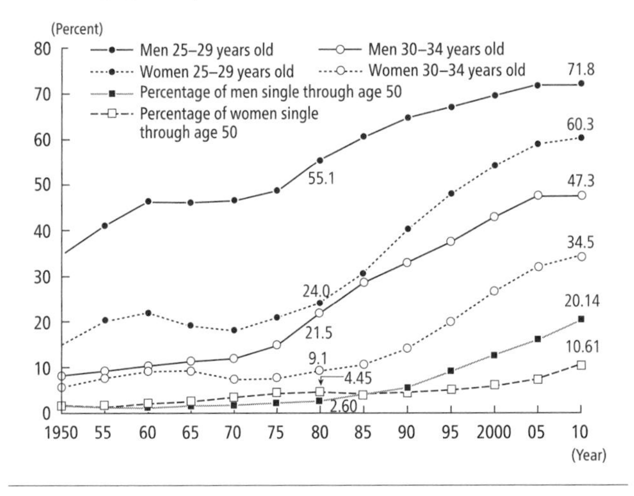

Source: Ministry of Health, Labour and Welfare, *Vital Statistics*.

The percentage of people who were unmarried in their early thirties was 5.7 percent for women and 8.0 percent for men in 1950, but today nearly half of the men and one-third of the women in that age group are unmarried. As a result, the birthrate has declined overall. Delayed marriage is one important cause of population decline and the decline in the birthrate, as is non-marriage—that is, the number of people who remain single throughout their lives—which is on the rise.

In 2015, the fact that the birthrate had recovered to 1.46 was considered newsworthy. It had been twenty-one years since the birthrate had exceeded 1.45 (it was 1.5 in 1994). But that is still a long way from the birthrate of 2.07 which is required to maintain a population at a given level. The number of deaths also exceeded the number of births in 2015, and the population declined by 280,000.

As for reasons why the decline in the birthrate is difficult to reverse, in addition to delayed marriage and non-marriage, here I would like to touch on the degradation of employment conditions for younger workers that began in the 1990s following the collapse of the bubble economy—that is, the increase in non-regular employment and the decline in wages. While 15 percent of employees were in non-regular employment in 1984, that figure increased to 37 percent in 2014 (Ministry of Health, Labour and Welfare, *Hiseiki koyō no genjō to kadai* [Current conditions and issues in non-regular employment]). Of course, employees in non-regular employment include some who have chosen part-time work as their preference. However, there are many employees who want to gain regular employment but reluctantly put up with non-regular employment since they cannot find regular, full-time jobs. Employees in non-regular employment not only suffer from employment insecurity, but their wages are also low. Comparing the marriage ratios of male workers (30–54 years old) in non-regular employment with those in regular employment, while the latter is 74 percent, the former is far lower at 36 percent (Ministry of Internal Affairs and Communications, *Rōdōryoku chōsa* [Labor force survey] 2014 average results). Sadly, economic difficulties are impeding marriage today.

The extension of life expectancy

In contemporary Japan, the number of people who cannot marry because of economic difficulties has increased, a harsh fact that recalls the era of Malthus. As Brentano points out, the birthrate has declined in the industrialized nations since the end the nineteenth century. What began to increase, as if in response to the decline in the birthrate, was average life expectancy. This point belies the predictions of Malthus. Malthus mockingly criticized Condorcet, who was optimistic about the extension of life expectancy: "it may be fairly doubted whether there is really the smallest perceptible advance in the natural duration of human life since first we have had any authentic history of man" (Malthus 1798, p. 50). Contradicting this assertion, life expectancies in industrialized nations have increased greatly during the twentieth century.

Japan has the longest or second-longest life expectancy in the world today. Nevertheless, this should not be taken for granted. The increase in average life expectancy of the Japanese people may be considered the greatest accomplishment achieved by postwar Japan. In 1950, just before Japan's high-growth period began, Japan had the shortest life expectancy among the industrialized nations! This is an important fact that many people today have forgotten.

"Snowflakes are letters sent from heaven."

This beautiful sentence is from the famous book *Yuki* (Snow) by Dr. Ukichirō Nakaya. Nakaya wrote his impressions from his travels in the U.S. in 1950, just five years after the war ended.

> What impressed me most on my visit to the U.S. this time was that there are many elderly people, and they are all hale and working in good health. I was amazed

> by everything from the beautification of the towns to the improvement of roads all the way to the corners of the countryside to the large numbers of automobiles, but above all I was amazed at how people were living long lives in good health. This is what I found most enviable. . . While there may be various debates about the extreme development of machine civilization, in fact the country in an uproar about the hydrogen bomb is the country that can make it, the U.S. Yet there is probably no one who opposes how science extends human life expectancy and makes it possible to maintain vigorous health in advanced age. In that sense, we should not allow our eyes to be drawn only to the developments of U.S. weapons and machines. We should pay more attention to the aspects where U.S. science is truly contributing to human happiness.
>
> (Nakaya 1950, "Rōreigaku: Nagaiki o suru gakumon no sonzai" [Gerontology: Existence of the science of longevity] in *Nakaya Ukichirō zuihitsu senshū dai 2 kan* [Collected essays of Ukichirō Nakaya, vol. 2]).

Nakaya discusses how Americans have great interest in vitamins, minerals, and nutrition, and suggests that Japanese should also learn scientific nutrition.

> This is because I was astonished by the statistics on the average life expectancy of Americans. In 1900 the average life expectancy in the U.S. was forty-seven years, but forty years later in 1940 it had suddenly grown to sixty-three years. The year 1940 was the year before the Pacific War broke out. Within the next two years U.S. average life

> expectancy increased further to 64.82 years in 1942. It is remarkable that this average life expectancy increased by 1.82 over just two years, while Japan was preoccupied with the developments from the Tripartite Pact and the fall of Singapore to the Naval Battle of Guadalcanal.
>
> (Nakaya 1950, op. cit.)

In the 1940s, when Nakaya visited the U.S., the average life expectancy was sixty-five years in the U.S. (1942) compared with fifty years for men and fifty-four years for women in Japan (1947).

Changes in average life expectancy in Japan

Let us review once again the shifts in average life expectancy in Japan. As mentioned previously, Japan has one of the longest average life expectancies in the world today. The average life expectancy in Japan in 2015, announced by the World Health Organization (WHO) in May 2016, was 83.7 years for the population as a whole, which was the longest in the world. Viewed separately by sex, the average life expectancy for men was 80.5 years—following Switzerland (81.3 years) and Iceland (81.2 years)—but for women it was 86.8 years, which was the longest in the world.

In this context, the number of people who live to be over 100 has been steadily increasing for nearly half a century. The number of centenarians in Japan, which was 339 in 1971, had increased to 58,820 by Respect for the Aged Day (Sept. 15) in 2014. The oldest was a 116-year-old woman who was recognized as the oldest person in the world in the 2013 Guinness

Book of World Records. Japan is indeed the longest-lived society in the world, but today, if we do not pay attention, we might come to view this fact as a matter of course. There are even some people who believe Japanese live long because we have eaten a lot of fish since ancient times.

Average life expectancy does not increase in a straight line in parallel with the development of medical technology. Although we are all human, there are countries and regions such as Japan and Hong Kong, and Iceland and other countries in Europe, where average life expectancy exceeds eighty years, while there are also countries such as Sierra Leone, Zambia, Swaziland, and the countries of equatorial Africa where average life expectancy is in the forties.

The average life expectancy of men in Russia during the late 1980s under the Soviet Gorbachev regime was sixty-four years, but this shortened by six years over just three years after the 1991 collapse of the Soviet Union, declining to 57.6 years in 1994. However, that subsequently recovered to sixty-three years as of 2013. In many countries, women have longer average life expectancies than men. In Tonga, as of 2013, however, men live longer, with an average life expectancy of seventy-three years compared to seventy years for women. In this way, average life expectancies are greatly influenced by social and economic conditions.

Chart 3-4 presents the shifts in average life expectancies for men and women in Japan and the U.S. from the twentieth century to the early twenty-first century. As shown by this chart, the average life expectancy in Japan increased very little over the first half of the twentieth century, prior to World War II; this is the fact that Nakaya lamented. After the war,

Chart 3-4. Changes in Average Life Expectancy in Japan and the U.S.

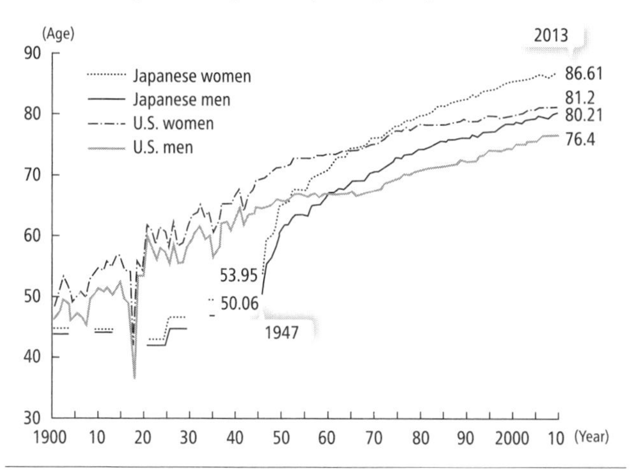

Sources: Ministry of Health, Labour and Welfare, *Complete Life Tables*, *Abridged Life Tables* (prior to World War II, *Complete Life Tables* only); National Vital Statistics Reports, *Historical Statistics of the United States*.

however, Japan's average life expectancy grew dramatically to surpass the other industrialized nations, becoming the longest in the world.

Life expectancy before World War II

Around the year 1900, the average life expectancy was forty-seven years in the U.S., forty-five years in the U.K., and forty-three years in Japan. So Japan's average life expectancy was a bit shorter compared to the U.S. and the U.K., but it was basically around the same level; there was no gap like the one that exists today between the industrialized countries and the nations of equatorial Africa.

Upon consideration, this might seem strange. If you look at the differences in average life expectancies in the world today, there is a strong correlation between average life expectancies and per capita income levels. In wealthy nations, average life expectancies are long, and conversely in poor countries they are short. In 1900, Japan's per capita income was very low compared with those of the U.S. and the U.K., which were at the top level worldwide. For example, according to research by Angus Maddison, who examined long-term global economic statistics, in 1900 Japan's per capita income was a fourth of England's, less than half of Argentina's—which was one of the few advanced nations in the world at the time—and lower than Chile's and Mexico's (Maddison 1995). Why was the average life expectancy in Japan, which was still among the poorer countries, around the same as that in the U.S. and the U.K., which were the richest nations in the world?

The leading theory is that it's because industrialization and urbanization happened much later in Japan than in the U.S. and the U.K. At first glance, this may also seem strange. During the nineteenth century, the economic development of the U.S., the U.K., and other advanced nations was brought about by industrialization, which moved them beyond the traditional agricultural economy. Industrialization simultaneously promoted urbanization: people left the agricultural villages of rural areas behind and flocked to the cities. As seen in chapter 2, such population migration occurred at a strikingly rapid pace in Japan during the high-growth era of the 1950s and 1960s.

Today, we tend to perceive cities as being advanced and

rural villages as being backward, but in fact, at the end of the nineteenth century, especially from the perspective of people's health, cities were far riskier places to live than rural villages. At a time when many communicable diseases were fatal due to the lack of public hygiene and the fact that medicines had not been developed, cities where people lived crowded together were extremely disadvantageous for the maintenance of health and long life.

It was under such conditions that Sōseki Natsume, who was studying in London at the turn of the century, wrote the following description.

> Take a walk in the city of London and try to spit out phlegm. You will be surprised to see a jet-black lump. Millions of citizens absorb this soot and dust each day, staining their lungs. When I blow my nose or spit out phlegm, it's so horrible that I don't want to do it.
>
> (*Sōseki zenshū dai 13 kan* [Collected works of Sōseki, vol. 13], "Diary," January 4, 1901)

During this period, even though income levels in the U.S., the U.K., and other advanced nations were high, the urbanization that they were experiencing was a disadvantage. In Japan, conversely, many people were still living in agricultural areas, which cancelled out the disadvantage of low income levels. This is why, as of 1900, the average life expectancy in Japan was not all that different from those in the U.S. and the U.K. Thus, at the beginning of the twentieth century, Japan was standing at the same starting line as other industrialized nations, which went on to experience a more or less straight-line increase in average life expectancy due to a rise in income levels, the progress of medicine, and the development of public hygiene. In chart 3-4, the U.S. is representative, but the pattern was similar in the U.K. and many other European countries.

In Japan, however, average life expectancy hardly changed over the first half of the twentieth century. According to the theory put forth by the demographers S. Ryan Johansson and Carl Mosk, this can be attributed to the fact that, while the Meiji government had worked toward achieving basic public hygiene, at the start of the twentieth century the government rushed to bolster military capabilities and neglected investment in waterworks, hospitals, and other infrastructure (Johansson and Mosk 1987). It must be said that, during the first half of the twentieth century, prewar Japan was a country with major problems related to health and life expectancy.

The neoliberal perspective on life expectancy

In contrast to this prewar stagnation, average life expectancy in Japan grew steadily after the war. Here, let me digress a bit to introduce the neoliberal perspective regarding life expectancy.

Some readers must be wondering what on earth neoliberalism, which is also called "market fundamentalism," has to do with life expectancy. Advocates of neoliberalism view individual choice in the market as all-important, and stress that the role to be played by government is generally small. They believe it is enough for government to do the minimum in such areas as national defense, the judiciary, and the police; the smaller the government, the better. Proponents of neoliberalism who hold these beliefs do not want to admit that public-hygiene improvements by the government contributed to the increase in average life expectancy. University of Chicago economic historian Robert Fogel, an advocate of neoliberalism who won the 1993 Nobel Prize in economics, insisted that the increase in life expectancy in industrialized nations in the twentieth century was basically the result of personal choices and actions taken voluntarily by individuals, such as consuming foods with high nutritional value that contribute to good health (Fogel 2004).

Many Japanese may view the neoliberal position, which does not recognize the government's role in public hygiene, to be an imbalanced and extreme theory. Neoliberalism may be considered uniquely American among the industrialized nations. The U.S. is also exceptional among the industrialized nations in not having national health insurance, even in the twenty-first century. The background to this lies in the thinking of the neoliberalists.

Of course, not all economists think that the smaller the role of government, the better. Angus Deaton, who won the 2015 Nobel Prize in economics, is representative of Fogel's critics. As already mentioned, Fogel claims that when people's incomes rise due to economic growth, they make choices and efforts to improve their own health, and consequently their average life expectancy increases. In contrast, Deaton says the extent to which rising incomes improve health is far smaller than people normally assume. In fact, in his book *The Great Escape*, Deaton stresses that knowledge is the most important factor for improving health and extending life expectancy. Unlike Fogel, Deaton does recognize the role of the government, but it seems this is overshadowed by knowledge. Yet while certainly important, "knowledge" is too abstract a term to encompass the experience of postwar Japan, as we are about to see.

The experience of postwar Japan

After World War II, average life expectancy in Japan steadily increased, in contrast to the prewar period. With the end of the war, tuberculosis—which had been an intractable disease—was conquered with the spread of penicillin and the BCG vaccine. Such advances in medicine made great contributions to longer life expectancy, but as Nakaya lamented when he visited the U.S. in 1950, the average life expectancy in Japan was then the lowest among the industrialized nations.

There were three reasons why life expectancy in Japan steadily increased after the war, as if to erase the dreary past of the prewar era. To name them in no particular order, one was the rise in average per capita income from economic growth; another was the progress of medicine and the efforts of doctors, nurses, and other medical personnel; and a third was the establishment (in 1961) of the National Health Insurance system covering all citizens.

The rise in income levels certainly contributed to the increase in average life expectancy, in line with the assertions of Fogel and neoliberalism, as people came to consume nutritious foods and live in airtight, warm housing. At this juncture, let us consider the infant mortality rate, which has a great influence on a country's average life expectancy, in some detail.

In the initial period of economic development from the nineteenth century through the early twentieth century, as far as health was concerned, cities were high-risk areas compared with rural villages. It was actually in the 1950s that the mortality rate in Japanese cities first fell below that in agricultural villages. This happened in the context of two developments: the impact of rising income levels on health became substantial, and the average income level became higher in the cities than in the countryside.

The changes around this time also had a large impact on the infant mortality rate. Chart 3-5 shows the shift in the infant mortality rate in Japan. This chart shows that there was a dramatic decline during the 1950s followed by further declines in the 1960s, and that the rate continued to fall

Chart 3-5. Changes in Japan's Infant Mortality Rate

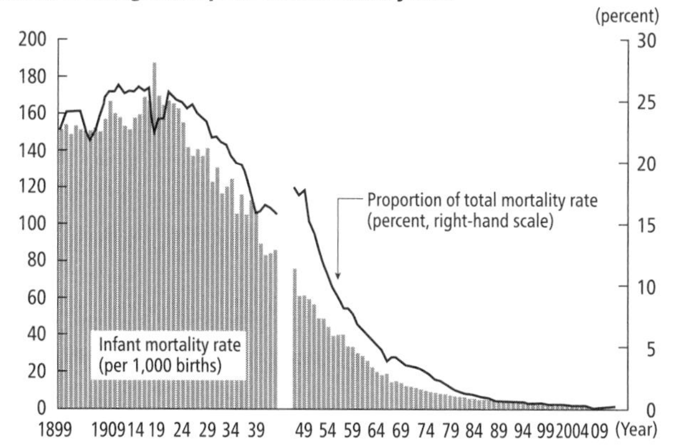

Source: Ministry of Health, Labour and Welfare, *Vital Statistics*.

further through the 1980s and has remained basically stable thereafter up to the present day. Researchers have noted different reasons for the decline in the infant mortality rate during each of those periods.

Regarding the high-growth period from 1950 through 1965, there is outstanding research by Seiritsu Ogura and Reiko Suzuki, who examined data by prefecture, city, and county in detail. This research found, first, that birth at hospitals and clinics decreased the infant mortality rate, and, second, that birth at such medical institutions rather than at home is greatly influenced by household income level as well as the mother's educational level.

Chart 3-6. 1947 Infant Mortality Rates by Prefecture (per 1,000 births)

Nationwide	76.7		
Hokkaido	82.8	Mie	88.7
Aomori	99.7	Shiga	86.9
Iwate	98.2	Kyoto	68.8
Miyagi	75.4	Osaka	79.9
Akita	97.0	Hyōgo	75.2
Yamagata	92.0	Nara	91.1
Fukushima	74.9	Wakayama	70.8
Ibaraki	81.2	Tottori	77.9
Tochigi	69.2	Shimane	76.0
Gunma	66.1	Okayama	80.0
Saitama	72.8	Hiroshima	67.9
Chiba	77.4	Yamaguchi	71.7
Tokyo	62.4	Tokushima	85.4
Kanagawa	60.3	Kagawa	81.5
Niigata	72.4	Ehime	75.6
Toyama	95.5	Kōchi	76.0
Ishikawa	86.9	Fukuoka	80.8
Fukui	85.9	Saga	95.8
Yamanashi	63.2	Nagasaki	80.6
Nagano	61.4	Kumamoto	70.0
Gifu	74.4	Ōita	87.5
Shizuoka	65.8	Miyazaki	73.6
Aichi	73.9	Kagoshima	74.1
		Okinawa	–

Source: Ministry of Health, Labour and Welfare, *Vital Statistics 2013*.

Whether at a hospital or a clinic, birth at a maternity ward is considered normal today. But even after the war in 1950, just before the high-growth period began, 97 percent of all births in Japan took place at home. Even in Tokyo, which had the highest percentage of births at medical institutions, the home birth rate was 78 percent. This is hard to believe today. The home birth rate declined throughout the high-growth period, and eventually the majority of births took place at medical institutions. Household income levels had a large impact on that popularization process. This fact may be said to disprove Deaton's assertion in *The Great Escape*, which is that income does not have much influence on the improvement of health.

There were large regional variations in the overall high infant mortality rate (chart 3-6) prior to the high-growth period. Be that as it may, the decline in the infant mortality rate greatly contributed to the increase in average life expectancy.

Establishment of the National Health Insurance system

The modern health insurance system is said to have been introduced by Otto von Bismarck, who was called the "Iron Chancellor," as a measure to counter emerging socialism in the German Empire at the end of the nineteenth century. In Japan, the Health Insurance Act was promulgated in 1922 to cover factory workers. Even after the war, however, in 1955 there was still no universal insurance covering all citizens; a third of the population, including farmers and the self-employed, had no health insurance. Japan's National Health Insurance system was established in 1961.

Chart 3-7 shows rates of disease prevalence, treatment, and mortality by age group in 1955. That the prevalence and mortality rates increase with age is probably just common sense. What is surprising, however, is that the treatment rate (the percentage of people examined by doctors at hospitals and clinics) declines with age. In every era the percentage of people suffering from illness is higher among the elderly compared with youth, but at medical institutions in 1955 the treatment rate of the elderly was lower. Subsequently, once the National Health Insurance system was established in 1961,

Chart 3-7. 1955 Distribution of Rates of Disease Prevalence, Treatment, and Mortality by Age Group

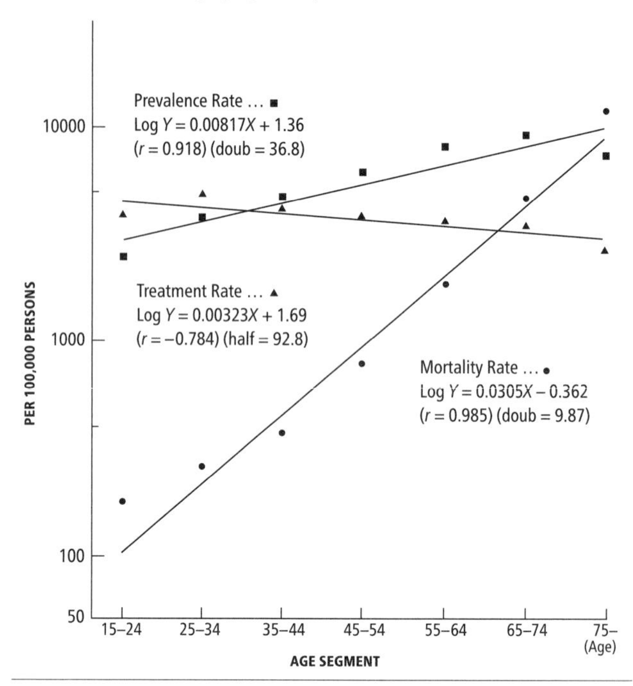

Source: Tatsuo Negishi and Masako Naitō, "Genjō to sono haikei kara mita 21 seiki no iryō seido" [The twenty-first century medical system seen from its current conditions and their background], in Hirofumi Uzawa (ed.), *Iryō no keizaigakuteki bunseki* [Economic analysis of healthcare].

the treatment rate of the elderly became higher than that of young people (chart 3-8). Apparently, before the National Health Insurance system was introduced, economic reasons were keeping many elderly people from seeking treatment even when they became ill. Today, excessive visits to doctors are seen as one factor causing the bloating of medical expenses; nonetheless, looking over Japan's postwar history from a long-term perspective, the National Health Insurance

Chart 3-8. Changes in Treatment Rates by Age Group

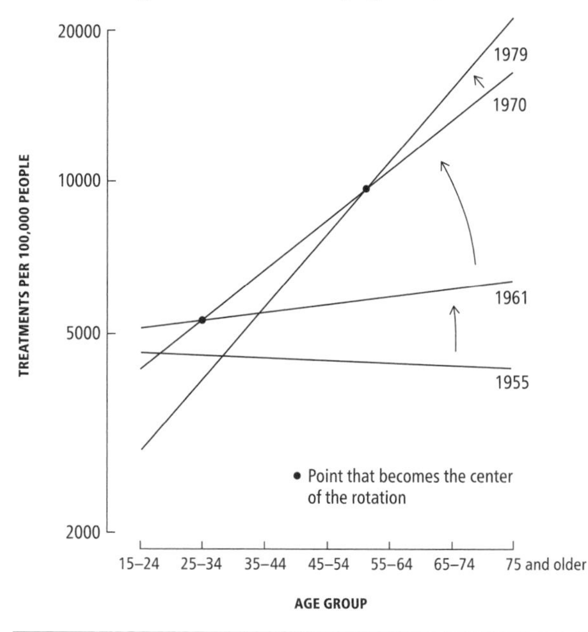

Source: Tatsuo Negishi and Masako Naitō, "Genjō to sono haikei kara mita 21 seiki no iryō seido" [The twenty-first century medical system seen from its current conditions and their background], in Hirofumi Uzawa (ed.), *Iryō no keizaigakuteki bunseki* [Economic analysis of healthcare].

clearly made important contributions to the increase in average life expectancy. Incidentally, in Hong Kong, which shares Japan's top ranking for life expectancy, there is a public health insurance system which covers most citizens, under which, when someone is hospitalized, regardless of what operations they undergo, the maximum daily co-payment is 100 Hong Kong dollars (about ¥1,400 or US$13 as of 2016). Japan's National Health Insurance system, which has contributed to the increase in average life expectancy, is facing severe financial problems due to the aging of society and low birthrates, as explained in the previous chapter.

The Gini coefficient

Whether measuring income or height, when some variance in quantity is distributed across a population, what type of index should be used to express the extent of inequality has long been debated. Today, the Gini coefficient, devised by the Italian economist Corrado Gini, is often used as a representative index.

As a specific example, let us consider the income inequality in a society consisting of 100 people. For that purpose, first, we assign the number 1 to the person with the lowest income and the number 100 to the person with the highest. These become the income ranks on the X-axis. Next, we check their income shares to determine what fraction of the society's total income comes from each individual's income. We set the Y-axis scale based on these income share figures from 1 to 100, adding them cumulatively. For example, if the income shares of the poorest three people are 1/500, 1/400, and 1/300, the first

Chart 3-9. Income Equality Gini Coefficient

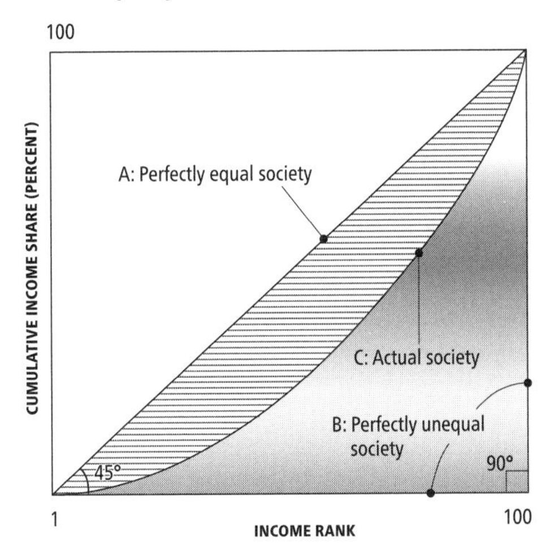

point on the Y-axis is 1/500. The second point, however, is not 1/400, but rather 1/500 + 1/400; similarly, the third point is 1/500 + 1/400 + 1/300. The income figures are "cumulatively" added moving up the Y-axis in this manner. The curve drawn from the resulting points is called a Lorenz curve.

It is easy to understand the Lorenz curve by looking at the extreme cases of perfect equality and perfect inequality. In a perfectly equal society, everyone's income is the same, so each person's income share is 1/100. In this case, the Lorenz curve will be the 45-degree straight line A shown on chart 3-9: the first point is 1/100; the second point 1/100 + 1/100 = 2/100; the third point 3/100, and so on.

Conversely, in the extreme example of a perfectly unequal society, the income of 99 out of 100 people is zero, while the 100th person alone receives all the society's income. In this case the Lorenz curve remains at zero from point 1 to point 99 (because the value of the income share on the Y-axis is zero, this is the same as the X-axis) and then suddenly jumps to a value of 1 (an income share of 100 percent) at point 100. This is represented by line B on chart 3-9. In the real world, the Lorenz curve resembles line C on chart 3-9, which is below the 45-degree line.

The Gini coefficient is defined as the area of the crescent-moon shape that is surrounded by the Lorenz curve and the 45-degree line divided by the area of the right-angled isosceles triangle which has the 45-degree line as its hypotenuse (chart 3-9). As explained above, in a perfectly equal society the Lorenz curve equals the 45-degree line, so in this case the crescent moon area would disappear and the area would be zero. Consequently, in a perfectly equal society, the Gini coefficient is zero. In a perfectly unequal society, the Lorenz curve would resemble line B on chart 3-9. In this case the "crescent moon" would equal the right-angled isosceles triangle itself,

Chart 3-10. Gini Coefficient by Country (2010)

Country	Gini
Chile	0.510
Mexico	0.466
China*	0.462
Turkey	0.417
U.S.	0.380
Portugal	0.345
U.K.	0.341
Greece	0.338
Japan	0.336
Spain	0.334
Australia	0.334
New Zealand	0.324
Italy	0.321
Canada	0.319
Ireland	0.313
South Korea	0.310
Poland	0.307
France	0.303
Switzerland	0.298
Germany	0.286
Netherlands	0.283
Luxembourg	0.271
Austria	0.269
Sweden	0.269
Finland	0.265
Belgium	0.264
Czech Republic	0.258
Norway	0.249
Iceland	0.246

*Data for China is for 2015.
Source: *OECD Income Inequality Update* (June 2014); data for China is from China's National Bureau of Statistics (2015).

and thus the Gini coefficient would be 1. In general, the Gini coefficient is between zero and 1, as is clear from line C on chart 3-9. The Gini coefficient approaches zero as inequality declines, and it approaches 1 as inequality rises.

The Gini coefficient varies by country and by era. There are countries and times when income distribution is equal; likewise, there are countries and times when income distribution is unequal. Today, as shown in chart 3-10, the Gini coefficient is 0.25 in Iceland, Norway, and Denmark, which are known for having equal societies. It is around 0.3 in Germany and France, 0.34 in Japan and the U.K., and 0.38 in the U.S. (2010, OECD). In developing countries, inequality is generally high. In Chile and Mexico, the Gini coefficient is around 0.5. Among the industrialized nations, the Gini coefficient is unusually high in the U.S., at a level near that of Turkey, which is a newly industrialized country.

In China, the National Bureau of Statistics has been announcing the Gini coefficient since the 2000s. As shown in chart 3-10, China's Gini coefficient was 0.462 in 2015, a slight decrease compared with 0.491 in 2008, but still high. Even today, inequality remains a serious problem in China, which is a socialist country.

In Japan, the Ministry of Health, Labour and Welfare calculates the Gini coefficient once every three years using the Comprehensive Survey of Living Conditions, and publishes the results. As shown in chart 3-11, the Gini coefficient rose from 1979 through 2009; that is to say, the level of inequality increased. However, caution is required when interpreting these results. This is because this Gini coefficient is calculated using "initial income," which does not include pensions. That

Chart 3-11. Japan's Various Gini Coefficients

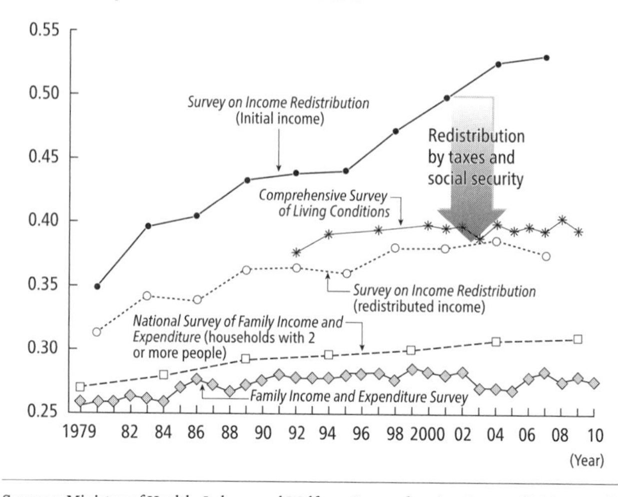

Sources: Ministry of Health, Labour and Welfare, *Comprehensive Survey of Living Conditions*; Ministry of Internal Affairs and Communications, *National Survey of Family Income and Expenditure*, and *Family Income and Expenditure Survey*.

causes the income figures to be significantly lower in the case of elderly persons for whom pensions are the pillar of their incomes. For that reason, the Gini coefficient using "redistributed income," which includes pensions in income, is also published. This is the Gini coefficient "after redistributions" shown in chart 3-11.

As shown in this chart, the Gini coefficient after redistributions is lower than the Gini coefficient based on initial income. The rate of increase is also more gradual. This indicates that Japan's aging population is a major reason why the Gini coefficient using initial income has risen. While Japan's national finances are in dire shape, as seen in chapter 2, pensions, healthcare, and other social security measures are

Chart 3-12. Long-Term Changes in the Gini Coefficient

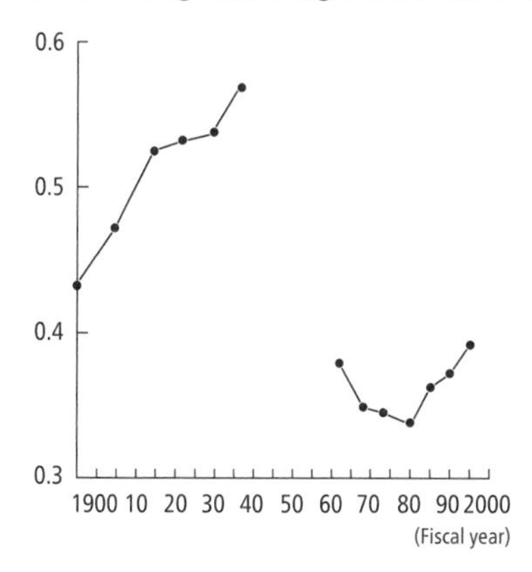

Source: Minami 2002.

Note: Figures for 1895, 1905 and 1915 are provisional estimates by Minami. Figures for 1923, 1930 and 1937 are estimates by Minami. Figures after WWII are estimates by Mizoguchi and Terasaki.

important for maintaining social equality in the era of the super-aged society. In addition to the Gini coefficient calculated using the Comprehensive Survey of Living Conditions, chart 3-11 also presents the Gini coefficient calculated using the National Consumption Conditions Survey and the Family Income and Expenditure Survey. It is worth noting that the latter figure is much lower than the Gini coefficient based on the Comprehensive Survey of Living Conditions, which is used more often.

What differences are there in the Gini coefficient before and after World War II? Many economists have amassed research regarding the distribution of income in prewar Japan. According to Minami (2002), as is clear from a glance at chart 3-12, prewar Japan was a far more unequal society than postwar Japan. The chart shows not only that the Gini coefficient was high before the war, but also that inequality rose conspicuously from 1900 through the 1930s.

Chart 3-13. Shifts in the Income Share of the Top 0.1 percent

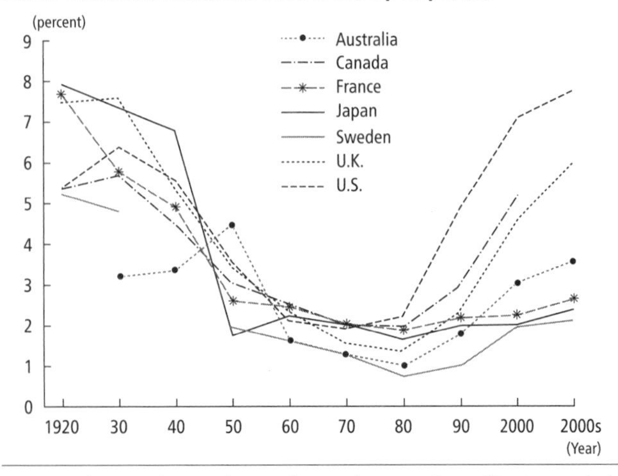

Source: Anthony B. Atkinson, Thomas Piketty, and Emmanuel Saez, "Top Incomes in the Long Run of History," *Journal of Economic Literature* 2011, 49:1, 3–71.

The "level of richness" of the super-rich

While the Gini coefficient is widely used as an index showing inequality, there is another popular measure, that is, the share of the top 1 percent (1/100) or top 0.1 percent (1/1,000) in the total income of an entire society—in other words, the "level of richness" of the super-rich.

The French economist Thomas Piketty, whose *Capital in the Twenty-First Century* was a bestseller when he visited Japan in 2015, uses this income share of the wealthy exclusively in discussing the income distribution problem.

Chart 3-13 by Piketty and his joint researchers shows the change in the income share of the top 0.1 percent from 1920 to 2010. From this chart, it is clear that in all of the industrialized nations, including Japan, the income share of the super-rich was extremely high prior to World War II. Before the war, some people were really fabulously wealthy.

An interesting fact is that after the war, this share suddenly dropped in both the countries that won the war and those that lost. The class that was wealthy before the war suffered a downfall. In Japan, such dramatic changes were brought about by the breakup of the *zaibatsu* business conglomerates, emancipation of farmland, freezing of deposits, hyperinflation, and wealth taxes. The dramatic decline in the income share of the wealthy corresponds naturally with the postwar decline in the Gini coefficient described above.

Looking at chart 3-13, we can see that a different trend emerged around 1980 in the industrialized nations. Especially in the U.S., the income share of the top 0.1 percent increased steadily, and rose so far that in 2000 it surpassed the prewar peak recorded in the 1920s and 1930s. The 1920s was the era in which Henry Ford, John D. Rockefeller, Andrew Carnegie, J.P. Morgan, and other legendary magnates lived. Surprisingly, in the U.S., the income share of the super-wealthy is now higher than it was during that time.

Amid the severe recession sparked by the bankruptcy of Lehman Brothers on September 15, 2008, "Occupy Wall Street" and other student and citizen movements protesting on behalf of the "99 percent"—that is, those who are not in the top 1 percent—gained force; this is understandable looking at chart 3-13. Such developments also explain the huge popularity of the English version of Piketty's *Capital in the Twenty-First Century*, which was published in the U.S. a bit later than the original French version. The income share of the top 0.1 percent rose in the U.K. as well, although not as much as it did in the U.S. This trend did not emerge in France or Japan, however—a point I will touch on once again in chapter 4.

Japan became a far more equal society after the war compared with before the war. What sort of relationship did this have with the shift in average life expectancy? Declines in infant mortality rates greatly contribute to increases in average life expectancy. As already seen, infant mortality rates relate strongly to income, especially up to a certain income level. Consequently, before the war, during the era when the average income in Japan was at the level of semi-developed countries, income inequality kept the infant mortality rate from falling.

The Gini coefficient of life expectancy

Average life expectancy is certainly an important indicator, but we can move a step further and look at the inequalities in life expectancies. This can be done by investigating the dispersion of the life expectancies of one million people born in the same year (i.e., a "cohort") with life spans ranging from death within one year of birth to death at age 100. If we grasp that, then exactly the same method used for the income distribution calculation can be used to calculate the Gini coefficient for the distribution of the lifespans of people born in the same year. The dispersion of life expectancies can be calculated by reviewing the number of people in the cohort who died each year.

The economist Sam Peltzman has been studying the "mortality Gini coefficient" created in this way, and his findings are of great interest. Chart 3-14 presents the changes in

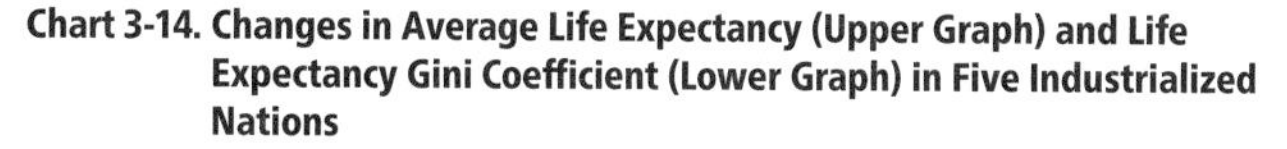

Chart 3-14. Changes in Average Life Expectancy (Upper Graph) and Life Expectancy Gini Coefficient (Lower Graph) in Five Industrialized Nations

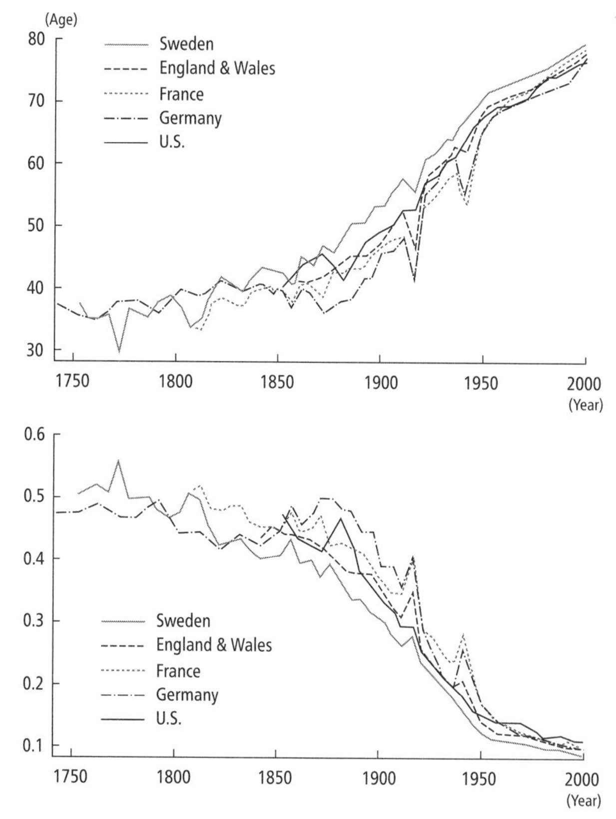

Source: Peltzman 2009, p. 180, figure 2.

average life expectancy and mortality Gini coefficient estimates for five industrialized nations for which statistics have long been available. While there are differences from country to country, the major changes are surprisingly similar. From the second half of the eighteenth century through the end of the nineteenth century, the mortality Gini coefficients were at a noticeably high level, from 0.5 to 0.4. This is far higher than the income-distribution Gini coefficients of the industrialized nations today. It is at the level of Latin American countries, where income distribution is remarkably unequal.

During that period, then, the inequality in life expectancy was greater than the income inequality. It was from the end of the nineteenth century through the first half of the twentieth century (up to around 1950) that a big change occurred in each country. During this period, the mortality Gini coefficient declined (that is, life expectancy leveled out) in parallel with a marked increase in average life expectancy. This trend also continued after the 1950s, but the change became much more gradual compared with that over the first half of the twentieth century.

Chart 3-15 presents the same data for five other countries, including Japan. The previous graph of five industrialized nations starts at 1750, but chart 3-15 begins at the end of the nineteenth century. The figures for the U.S. are reproduced for comparison purposes. Looking at Japan, which is our concern, the average life expectancy at the end of the nineteenth century was forty-six years. It was the highest among the nations of this group and the closest to the U.S. figure. Prior to World War II, however, as mentioned above, Japan stood out from the other countries because life expectancy there did not increase; in the 1940s life expectancy in Japan was surpassed by that in the U.S.S.R.

On the other hand, before the war Japan's mortality Gini

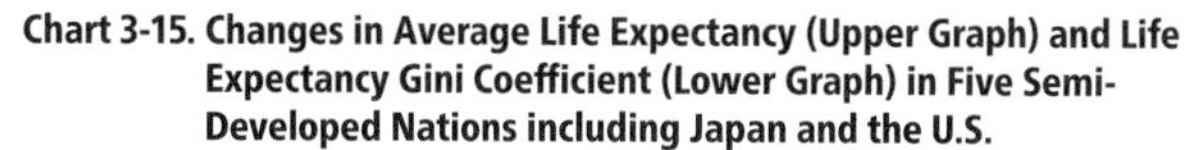

Chart 3-15. Changes in Average Life Expectancy (Upper Graph) and Life Expectancy Gini Coefficient (Lower Graph) in Five Semi-Developed Nations including Japan and the U.S.

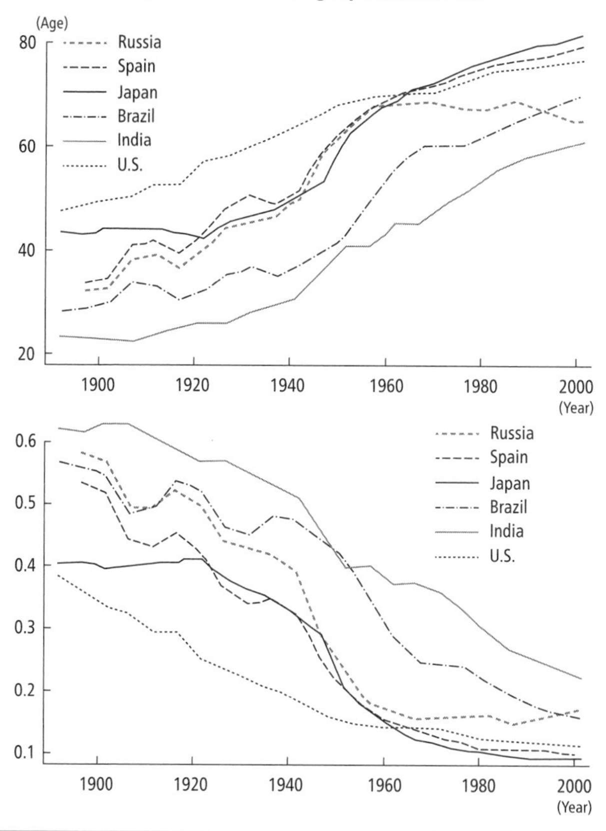

Source: Peltzman 2009, p. 185, figure 3.

coefficient was 0.4, which was the lowest in this group. It remained at that level until around the time of the Great Kantō Earthquake (1923). The mortality Gini coefficient finally began to decline in the 1930s. In this sense, too, there was a large problem in Japanese society before the war. In the five industrialized nations seen in chart 3-14, the increase in average life expectancy and the decline in the Gini coefficient of life expectancy become gradual after 1950. In the semi-developed countries shown in chart 3-15, however, large changes can be seen after 1950. The average life expectancy in Japan surpassed that in the U.S. starting around 1964. This was just 15 years after Nakaya returned from the U.S. and lamented the short average life expectancy in Japan.

To digress, the changes in the average life expectancy and Gini coefficient figures in the U.S.S.R./Russia are most interesting. From after the 1917 revolutions until the second half of the 1950s, the average life expectancy steadily increased in the U.S.S.R., as it did in Japan and Spain. The Gini coefficient also steadily declined. However, a conspicuous stagnation began in the late 1950s. Average life expectancy did not increase at all; in fact, it grew shorter. At the same time, the Gini coefficient rose! The Soviet Union collapsed in 1991, but from the average life expectancy and Gini coefficient figures, one can see how the problems with the socialist system emerged in the 1950s and brought the society to an impasse. The Soviet Union simply self-destructed.

As Brentano had discovered 100 years earlier, the population of industrialized nations began to decline amid wealth, even as life expectancy had started to increase conspicuously. But in the first half of the twentieth century—that is, prior to

World War II—life expectancy in Japan did not increase at all, making Japan an exception among the industrialized nations.

There are people who assert that prewar Japan was not as "bad" a society as others sometimes say. And indeed, it is rare for a single society to be bad in all ways. If you look, you will certainly find some positive aspects. However, considering the levels of the average life expectancy, which may be called the final account of human society, and the Gini coefficient, it must be said that prewar Japan was a society that had great problems.

Life expectancy in postwar Japan suddenly increased, in stark contrast to the prewar period, and Japan became the nation with the longest life expectancy in the world. This was the greatest accomplishment of postwar Japan.

What Does Economics Mean for People?

In the eighteenth century, Malthus and Smith accepted as a premise that if people become wealthy, they will have many children. In the world of living organisms, it is common sense that numbers grow when food supply increases. But as we saw in the last chapter, population in industrialized nations began to decline amid wealth at the end of the nineteenth century. Meanwhile, instead of a population increase, it was average life expectancy that grew at an unprecedented rate.

Per capita income affects both population and life expectancy. As explained in chapter 2, innovation is the factor that causes per capita income to rise. Innovation has created a wealthy society. Yet in this wealthy society the population is not increasing, as Malthus thought, but has begun to decline.

What exactly is wealth? In this chapter, let us consider such issues as what economics means for people, and how to define economic growth. But first, we must begin with the question of what economics is.

Economics and luxury

So, what is economics? If formally asked this question, one answer might be as follows.

Each individual person lives, as an organism, by means of physiological metabolism. It is the role of medicine and physiology to clarify such life mechanisms. But even if the physiological mechanisms that maintain the life of one human being are understood, whether that individual can go on living is a different matter. Regardless of how tough one's body may be, anyone left alone in the desert can only wait for death. Even Einstein could not live alone. Humans can only gain the energy required for existence collectively. Not only humans, but other organisms that are somewhat evolved also act collectively to some extent or another; for example, to protect themselves from external enemies and to obtain food. Economics is none other than this "collective metabolism" carried out by humans.

Unlike in the cases of honeybees, lions, and fish, however, the economic activities of human beings go beyond the bare minimum for survival as a species. On the contrary, as everyone knows, they are conducted at a level that far surpasses such a minimum. While this tendency is largely related to the important issue of "Is economic growth necessary?" examined later on, it has been noted since before the eighteenth century, when modern economic growth began.

For example, in William Shakespeare's *King Lear*, which was first performed in 1606, the old king rails against his daughters who have betrayed him.

> O, reason not the need! Our basest beggars
> Are in the poorest thing superfluous.

Allow not nature more than nature needs,
Man's life is cheap as beast's. Thou art a lady;
If only to go warm were gorgeous,
Why, nature needs not what thou gorgeous wear'st,
Which scarcely keeps thee warm.

(Act 2, Scene 4)

The moral viewpoint that luxury is a vice and simplicity a virtue has long existed in both the East and the West. It was the heretical philosopher Bernard Mandeville (1670–1733) who argued directly against such traditional values by asserting that it is vice itself that brings about a nation's prosperity. *The Fable of the Bees* (1714), which was published 100 years after Shakespeare, had an unusual format with just twenty pages of poetry, "notes" exceeding 200 pages, and a "dialogue" of more than 300 pages. In this book, Mandeville discloses his own socioeconomic philosophy, which is that vices like luxury and extravagance bring prosperity to a country's economy and society.

In the world of the bees of the title, the bees are grumbling while buzzing their wings.

The Root of Evil, Avarice,
That damn'd ill-natur'd baneful Vice,
Was Slave to Prodigality,
That noble Sin; whilst Luxury
Employ'd a Million of the Poor,
And odious Pride a Million more:
Envy it self, and Vanity,
Were Ministers of Industry;

Their darling Folly, Fickleness,
In Diet, Furniture and Dress,
That strange ridic'lous Vice, was made
The very Wheel that turn'd the Trade.
Their Laws and Clothes were equally
Objects of Mutability.

The bees are living flamboyantly in this way when one day they suddenly want to eliminate the vice in their hypocritical hearts. When Jupiter learns of this, he angrily grants their wish, and all vices are completely swept from the hive. And then, what do you think happens? The prosperity that was everywhere suddenly disappears!

The Shew is gone, it thins apace;
And looks with quite another Face.
For 'twas not only that They went,
By whom vast Sums were Yearly spent;
But Multitudes that liv'd on them,
Were daily forc'd to do the same.
In vain to other Trades they'd fly;
All were o'er-stock'd accordingly.
The Price of Land and Houses falls;
Mirac'lous Palaces, whose Walls,
Like those of *Thebes*, were rais'd by Play,
Are to be let; while the once gay,
Well-seated Household Gods would be
More Pleas'd to expire in Flames, than see
The mean Inscription on the Door
Smile at the lofty ones they bore.

The building Trade is quite destroy'd,
Artificers are not employ'd.

Mandeville says that a world without the vices of luxury and extravagance is like a windmill in a region with no wind.

Unsurprisingly, Mandeville's *The Fable of the Bees* was banned in its time. Nevertheless, *The Fable of the Bees* was a forerunner of the new trend of thought that emerged in England in the eighteenth century, written half a century before Adam Smith's *Wealth of Nations* (1776). In his *General Theory* (chapter 23), Keynes devotes three pages to *The Fable of the Bees*. From the perspective of Keynes' "principle of effective demand" that the state of the economy is determined by none other than demand, Mandeville is certainly a forerunner of Keynesian economics. In its view that luxury and extravagance move the economy, Mandeville's way of thinking was not by any means unique to eighteenth-century England. The economist Werner Sombart (1863–1941), who led the German Historical School, wrote a book entitled *Liebe, Luxus und Kapitalismus* (Love, luxury, and capitalism). In this book, Sombart develops the very clear-cut argument, as suggested by the title, that luxury generated and has been the driving force of the economic system called capitalism, and that if one searches for the origin of luxury, one finds that it is romance, which is led by women.

Some may disagree with Sombart's theory that love moves the economy. Yet it is clear to everyone that human economic activities go far beyond the bare minimum required for existence as living organisms. King Lear already cried out about this at the start of the seventeenth century. The fact that we have religious and ethical teachings from long ago that decry luxury and preach honorable poverty indicates there was already an awareness of the existence of excessive luxury in ancient times.

In what sense are excessive economic activities excessive? Let us revisit this essential question later on, and first explain how economic activity is measured.

The activity level of a nation's economy: Measurement of GDP

Individual economic activities—that is, consumption—are generally determined by a person's income. In discussions of income, monthly salaries were once used exclusively, but annual salaries are used more often these days. I say economic activities are "generally" determined by income because, while income is gained monthly or annually (this is called "flow"), a person's consumption also depends on his assets (which are not flow, but rather "stock"). As explained in chapter 2, using water in a swimming pool as a metaphor, assets are the quantity of water in the pool at a given point in time, while flow is the amount of water that flows in and out of the pool over a given period of time. These two are related, but they are different concepts. Income and consumption are flow, but assets are holdings, whether consisting of land or other real estate, or financial assets like savings deposits and stocks.

The above discussion is at the level of one person or one household, but the same applies to the economy as a whole. "National wealth" is one measure of a nation's assets, which are stock, but here let us consider how much economic value the economy generates each year. This is expressed as gross domestic product (GDP).

Older readers may remember that the term GNP was formerly used. GNP, which stands for gross national product, is slightly different from GDP, which is used today. GNP adds together all the economic value generated by Japanese people and Japanese enterprises over one year, regardless of whether the place where the economic value is generated is within Japan or overseas. In contrast, GDP adds together all the economic value generated within Japan over one year, regardless of whether it is created by Japanese people and enterprises or by foreign people and enterprises. For example, the income of Japanese professional athletes playing in the U.S. is included in Japan's GNP, but not in its GDP. Meanwhile, the profit of an enterprise in Japan that is owned by foreign capital is not included in Japan's GNP, but it is included in Japan's GDP. Today, GDP is the measure that is used internationally and in Japan as well.

Whether GNP or GDP, the idea of adding together all the economic value generated by the Japanese economy over one year is not particularly difficult as a concept. It should be easy to understand. But to do so is easier said than done. Producing this one figure of GDP is by no means simple.

While attempts to generate statistics corresponding to what we call GDP today go back to William Petty in the seventeenth century, full-scale efforts began at the end of the nineteenth century in Britain. Britain enjoyed economic prosperity under Queen Victoria after winning the Napoleonic Wars in 1815, but Germany and the U.S., which were then emerging economies, caught up as early as the 1870s. At that time, while there were production volume statistics on steel, textiles, and other goods, as well as customs statistics on trade, there was no scale to measure the size of the entire economy. Efforts began in Britain to prepare GDP statistics (although the term GDP was not used at that time) in order to answer such questions as how large the British economy was compared with those of Germany and the U.S., and how fast it was growing. The GDP framework was finally arranged during World War II by two students of Keynes: Richard Stone (1913–91, Nobel Prize in economics 1984) and James Meade (1907–95, Nobel Prize in economics 1977). This has been improved on ever since that time; the work is presently conducted by the United Nations.

An incomplete but useful index

GDP combines all the economic value—strictly speaking the "value added"—generated in one country over one year, but there are many points that should be noted here. For one, in "economic value" GDP includes only goods and services subject to market transactions. Housework inside the household is not reflected in GDP figures. Consequently, if a meal is prepared inside the home, GDP does not change, but if the same meal is eaten out, GDP increases by that amount. And when parents provide childcare for their own children, GDP is unaffected, but when the children are placed in a nursery, GDP increases. These points may be unsatisfactory if we try to use GDP as a measure of our welfare.

When one looks more closely, there are many even stranger aspects. For example, if there is an outbreak of influenza in the winter, the consequent medical expenses increase the GDP, and if beautiful oceans and rivers, blue sky, and clean air are lost and environmental countermeasures are implemented for mitigation, GDP increases even when the environment is not returned to its original state.

Seeing such examples, one might think that GDP is a very poor measure that does not stand up to use. To be certain, it is important to understand the limitations of GDP. But GDP is far too valuable a statistic to discard out of hand. Just as the population of a nation is important to know when seeking clues to resolve various problems, the size of a nation's economy is also indispensable information in our complex contemporary economic system. Therefore, as already

Chart 4-1. Per Capita GDP and Average Life Expectancy (2010)

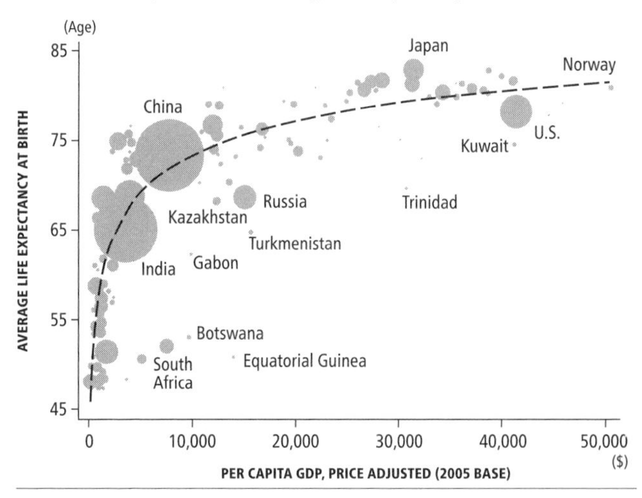

Source: A. Deaton, *The Great Escape*.

Note: The size of the circles inside the chart is proportional to population.

mentioned, the measurement of GDP has been refined by the efforts of a great many people across five centuries, and those improvements are still ongoing.

GDP is an incomplete measure of our welfare. But anyone can understand the significance of GDP by seeing the clear positive relationship between per capita GDP and average life expectancy presented in chart 4-1. There are some divergent opinions regarding the relationship between per capita income and average life expectancy, as stated by Deaton in *The Great Escape*, quoted in the previous chapter. Regardless, I adopt the straightforward interpretation that higher income promotes health and extends average life expectancy through a variety of channels.

What is economic growth?

GDP is terribly incomplete as a measurement of our welfare and happiness, but as is clear from chart 4-1, it is still an economic indicator that cannot be ignored. GDP growth is none other than economic growth. If the GDP was 100 the previous year and increased to 102 this year, then the economic growth rate was 2 percent.

I have one indelible memory regarding the GDP. This incident happened more than twenty years ago. I was on the way back from a university meeting that had continued until late at night, and a science professor who was rushing home with me along the same route suddenly asked me a question. He said, "All things considered, economics is rather strange. While energy remains constant regardless of what human beings do, how is it that the GDP increases?" To be sure, if one views the economic activities carried out by humans as physical phenomena, as long as one considers kinetic energy, potential energy, heat, electric energy, and all other forms of energy, the total energy remains constant regardless of what people do. Despite that, GDP does grow larger.

The reason for this becomes clear if we remember how GDP is defined. GDP assigns a value to each of the goods and services that we produce in one year and adds them all together. The prices that we use as standards of value express subjective human assessment. Let us consider cooking as an example. No matter how you heat the food or change the seasoning, its energy remains unchanged. Yet the prices of the resulting cooked meal vary widely. If we humans feel something tastes so good that we will pay a high price for it, it will cost more. Conversely, if people feel it has less value, then the price becomes low. The GDP and the prices on which it is based are subjective scores that humans assign to goods and services. In this sense, economics is truly human-centered.

When one says human-centered, some may think it is therefore selfish, but economics is not the only field that is human-centered. To begin with, without a human-centered orientation, the very concept of "illness" would not exist. Viewed as physical and chemical phenomena, when illness and death occur, the energy remains unchanged, and there is no "abnormality" with those phenomena. That is because in the human body as well, there is nothing that violates the laws of physics or chemistry. What makes illness and death a problem despite that is, of course, the human-centered viewpoint—in other words, the fact that humans see these phenomena as negative. Without being human-centered, the science of medicine would not exist. From this standpoint, it is not unusual that humans assign "numbers" (i.e., prices) based on subjective values to various goods and services—including, of course, medical treatment

Just as GDP, which is a subjective "total score," can increase even though energy remains constant, it also sometimes declines. In fact, Japan's nominal GDP fell from ¥523 trillion in 1997 to ¥471 trillion in 2011. Regardless, the GDP of industrialized nations, including Japan, has increased as a long-term trend since the Industrial Revolution of the eighteenth century.

What causes GDP to grow? As explained in chapter 2, increases in GDP are definitely not brought about by increases in population. Looking back at Japan's economic growth over the 100 years after the Meiji Restoration (1868), it is clear that GDP growth has virtually no relation with population dynamics (chart 2-6 in chapter 2). As Joseph Schumpeter discerned, it is innovation that drives economic growth in industrialized nations, and as a result, per capita GDP rises.

The issue lies in the nature and content of the innovation that generates economic growth. The most important role is played by product innovation, which creates new goods and services. But before explaining that conclusion, I will first discuss factors that hinder economic growth in industrialized nations.

Saturation of demand

The demand for existing goods and services always becomes saturated. This reality, which should be called a law, is a

January 30, 1931: Joseph Schumpeter, who gave a lecture at the University of Tokyo (third from right). Photographed in front of the Yasuda Auditorium. Eijirō Kawai is on Schumpeter's left; to his left is Seiichi Tōbata. (Tōbata Memorial Library collection)

fundamental factor that restricts the growth of industrialized nations. Initially demand—and with it, production volume—shows high growth, but the growth inevitably slows eventually. In extreme cases, beyond suffering a slowdown in demand, some goods and services are eliminated by what Schumpeter calls "creative destruction" and disappear altogether. Coal for heating is a typical example.

Japan's consumer price index (CPI), prepared by the Statistics Bureau of the Ministry of Internal Affairs and Communications, revises its base date every five years, considering changes in the consumption structure, and the list of goods included is also revised (chart 4-2). The goods and services that disappeared from this list are obviously goods and

Chart 4-2. Consumer Price Index (CPI) Main Items Added and Removed by Base Year

YEAR BASE	MAIN ITEMS ADDED	MAIN ITEMS REMOVED
1960	Lactic acid bacteria beverages, rent (public housing), rice cookers, toasters, televisions, refrigerators, lipstick, television subscription fees, cameras, lodging fees	Matches, straw paper, ink
1965	Instant ramen, cheese, lettuce, mayonnaise, bananas, strawberries, instant coffee, vacuum cleaners, wrist-watches, propane gas	Pinto beans, sesame seeds, insecticide powder, radio reception fees
1970	Instant curry, lemons, melons, cola, televisions (color), air conditioners, air fares, passenger cars, automobile gasoline, bowling fees, film (color), driving-school fees	Dried gourds, jackets, firewood, cotton flannel, serge, student caps
1975	Frozen foods, grapefruits, stereos, tape recorders, cellophane wrap, blue jeans, toilet paper, cram-school fees	Whale meat, synthetic sake, sewing machines (pedal operated)
1980	Beef (imported), oranges, potato chips, microwave ovens, beds, tissue paper, drinkable preparations, portable calculators, monthly tuition (swimming)	Televisions (black and white), charcoal, telegram fees, film (black and white)
1985	Room air conditioners (both heating and cooling), massage fees, shipping charges (home delivery), videotape recorders, pet food, monthly tuition (music)	Discount rice, sweetened beans, coal briquettes, shipping fees (railway)
1990	Broccoli, hamburgers, mop rental fees, contact lenses, word processors, video cameras, compact discs, video software rental fees	Cauliflower, *karintō* (deep-fried dough with brown sugar), sand, coal, brooms, fountain pens, records
1995	Foreign rice, pizza (delivered), water purifiers, air fresheners, passenger cars (imported), gasoline (premium), telephones, soccer match admission tickets	Fish sausages, caramel, plywood, toilet paper
2000	Mineral water, low-malt beer, bidet toilet seats, complete medical examination fees, mobile phone communications fees, personal computers, overseas packaged tours, tuition (English conversation), hair coloring, elder-care facility fees	Washing machines (two-tub), tape recorders, portable calculators, monthly tuition (abacus)
2005	Shōchū cocktails, dietary supplements, car navigation systems, mobile telephones, televisions (flat screen), DVD recorders, fitness club fees, beauty treatment fees	Designated standard rice, sewing machines, videotape recorders, pencils, monthly tuition (dressmaking)
2010	Salad dressing, disposable diapers (adult use), vaccinations, highway-bus fees, in-vehicle ETC devices, electronic dictionaries, pet grooming fees, memory cards	Kettles, Japanese sandals, television repair fees, photo albums, film
2015	Coffee beverages (self-service type at convenience stores), air purifiers, hearing aids, electric assist bicycles, pet toilet products	Lemons, kids' meals, plasterer fees, in-vehicle ETC devices

Source: Statistics Bureau, Ministry of Internal Affairs and Communications, *Outline of the Consumer Price Index*.

services eliminated by creative destruction. The goods and services that were newly added to this list are the fruits of product innovation.

In this way, there are goods and services for which both demand and production begin to decline, causing them to eventually disappear from the market. In many cases, the demand for goods and services, and consequently the production, initially increases over time. Nevertheless, the growth rate eventually slows to zero, ultimately reaching a ceiling. This means that the growth path is not an exponential function that expands forever at a fixed rate, as is often assumed in economic theory, but rather it follows an S-shaped "logistic curve." The growth rate of a logistic curve accelerates at first, but it eventually reaches the inflection point and then declines toward zero, thereby forming an S shape overall.

Regarding the idea of demand being equivalent to production for actual goods and services, a great deal of empirical research has been conducted concerning the "life cycle" of growth. For example, the engineers J.C. Fisher and R.H. Pry proposed a model in which the substitution of new goods for old goods is a key concept. Under this model, the growth of newly released goods follows a logistic curve. Fisher and Pry applied this model to natural rubber, synthetic rubber, and a variety of manufactured products, and demonstrated that, in fact, the growth of many goods follows a logistic curve. Chart 4-3 applies a standardized logistic curve with a ceiling of 1 to various goods that appeared in the U.S. over a period of almost 100 years. At a glance, one can see that the growth of many goods follows this pattern.

Papers that verify the research of Fisher and Pry in Japan

Chart 4-3. Logistic Curve (from the Fisher-Pry substitution model)

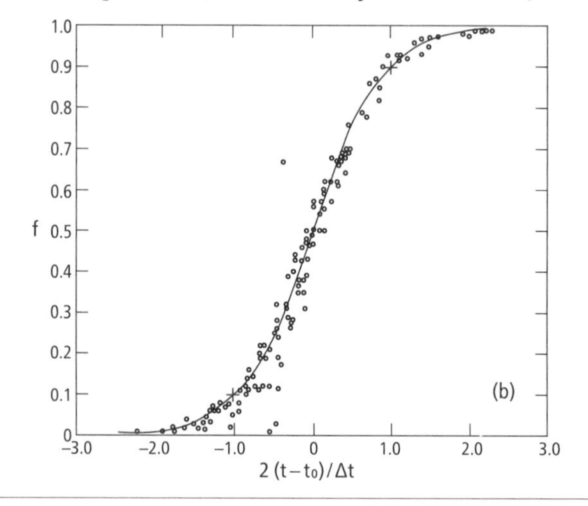

Source: Fisher and Pry 1971, p. 87, figure 9 (b).

include the series of papers by Masaaki Hirooka (Hirooka 2003). For details, see the Addendum at the end of this chapter.

Engel's Law

What Fisher and Pry, and Hirooka, investigated was primarily saturation of demand in the manufacturing industry, but economists have been noting the "saturation of demand" for a long time. The most famous of these observations is Engel's Law, which the German statistician Ernst Engel (1821–96) compiled using a household income survey in Belgium in 1895. This well-known maxim states that the wealthier the household, the smaller the percentage of consumption expenditures spent on food (the Engel coefficient). This holds true at all times and in all countries. When the consumption behavior of many households in a given society is investigated for a given year—which is what Engels did—Engel's Law holds true. Furthermore, on a macroeconomic level, when two countries with different levels of per capita income (such as Japan and China) are compared, we can see the relationship discovered by Engel: Japan, which has a higher income level than China, has a lower Engel coefficient than China does. Similarly, when conditions within Japan during the Meiji era are compared with the modern day, Engel's Law also holds true. In this way, Engel's Law is one of the few "laws" of economics that is truly deserving of that title.

Incidentally, what this law means is that the demand for food becomes saturated. This is because of the simple fact that there are physiological limits to the food demand of one human being. Regardless of how expensive meals—even fancy French cuisine—may be, the demand is ultimately constrained by the physical limits of the stomach.

Because the demand for food and thus for agriculture—the industry that produces food—becomes saturated, economic growth beyond that demand is led by industries other than agriculture; that is, by manufacturing and services. As a result, if per capita income increases, the market share of agriculture inevitably declines. In other words, Engel's coefficient declines. As mentioned above, when the demand for food becomes saturated, Engel's Law is upheld.

Downward pressure on mature economies

The law of demand saturation that Engel discovered concerning food clearly applies to goods other than food. As Fisher and Pry, and Hirooka, discovered, demand for any good will inevitably become saturated.

This most important fact for economics has been noted by great economists in the past. David Robertson, a friend of Keynes who became the professor of economics at Cambridge University after Arthur Cecil Pigou—at that time there was only one professor of economics at Oxford and Cambridge—in April 1930 expressed his own thoughts about the oncoming Great Depression at the MacMillan Committee, which had been established by the British government.

Robertson cited "the gluttability of wants" (i.e., the saturation of demand) as the main cause of the Great Depression. He then said that this problem is "at once the most fundamental, the most difficult to analyze, and the most difficult to counteract." When the demand for large numbers of goods and services is saturated, the economy falls into a major recession. To overcome this, he said, there is no choice but "the perpetual stimulation of new wants." Robertson, who had a touch for irony, continued in his somewhat cynical style as follows.

> Certainly the nation that has practiced this immoral art with most assiduity is that which has longest postponed the disease of industrial depression.

Robertson uses the verb "postpone" rather than "solve" in the belief that even if the stimulation of wants continues, in the end the economy cannot overcome the saturation of demand

and thereby avoid the eventual onset of economic depression.

Several years after Robertson's testimony, Keynes also wrote about the saturation of demand in his *General Theory*:

> Ancient Egypt was doubly fortunate, and doubtless owed to this its fabled wealth, in that it possessed two activities, namely, pyramid-building as well as the search for the precious metals, the fruits of which, since they could not serve the needs of man by being consumed, did not stale with abundance. The Middle Ages built cathedrals and sang dirges. Two pyramids, two masses for the dead, are twice as good as one; but not so two railways from London to York. Thus, we are so sensible, have schooled ourselves to so close a semblance of prudent financiers, taking careful thought before we add to the "financial" burdens of posterity by building them houses to live in, that we have no such easy escape from the sufferings of unemployment.

The benefits generated by the pyramids of ancient Egypt and the cathedrals of the Middle Ages do not decrease, regardless of how many are built. Consequently, the demand is never saturated. But in the economies of contemporary industrialized nations, the demand for existing goods and services always becomes saturated. In this way, the economy is chronically troubled by demand deficiency.

Even if such goods and services are produced, they will not sell (i.e., there is no demand), so companies do not make them. This leads to unemployment. What lies behind Keynesian economics—which asserts the "principle of effective demand," that it is aggregate demand that determines the economic activities of a nation—is the fact that the demand for existing goods and services inevitably becomes saturated.

Product innovation

If the demand for existing goods and services becomes saturated, then as long as the list of goods and services does not change, the growth of the economy overall will converge toward zero. In a mature economy, where many goods and services have become widespread, there is always downward pressure on economic growth. While this is only natural, the source of growth in the economies of such industrialized economies is the birth of new goods and services that enjoy high demand growth; in other words, "product innovation."

Demand saturation: this is where the economics of Keynes and Schumpeter, which are usually thought of like oil and water, suddenly come together. Keynes argues that the government should utilize public investment and low interest rates to overcome recessions caused by insufficient demand, while Schumpeter argues that the key to overcoming low growth from demand saturation is innovation.

In fact, the global automobile industry, including the industry in Japan, is now being led by new types of automobiles such as hybrid cars, electric vehicles, and intelligent vehicles. Japan's automobile industry originally established itself as a global leader because resource constraints and fuel efficiency became global issues in the 1970s. The Japanese automobile industry became a global front-runner through innovation that responded to such issues. Those conditions remain unchanged today.

If there were no product innovation that created new types of automobiles, and only conventional gasoline-powered automobiles were made, demand would certainly be determined by population. The saturation of demand stressed by Robertson and Keynes would definitely take effect. It is important to note that the term “demand” used here does not refer to the number of vehicles alone, but rather to the total value of the demand, which is the price per vehicle times the number of vehicles. In response to the needs of the times, new types of automobiles are generating new growth; this does not have a one-to-one correspondence with population.

There are countless other examples; for instance, disposable diapers. When someone mentions “diapers,” everyone thinks of diapers for babies, but sales of diapers for children have topped out with the declining birthrate. There would have been no outlook for future growth in disposable diaper production, but someone came up with the idea of disposable diapers for adults. Adult diapers did not involve any innovation in production technology. This was truly just product innovation on the demand side. As the aging of society has continued, the demand for adult diapers has increased rapidly, and in 2012 the value of adult diapers surpassed those of diapers for children (chart 4-4).

Limited express trains were originally used only for transportation to vacation spots, but certain railway companies decided to run them for long-distance commuting as well. People were willing to pay express fares for reserved seats rather than spending long commute times on packed trains. The limited express train, which addressed the needs of such people, is also unmistakably a product innovation. With the

Chart 4-4. Disposable Diaper Shipments

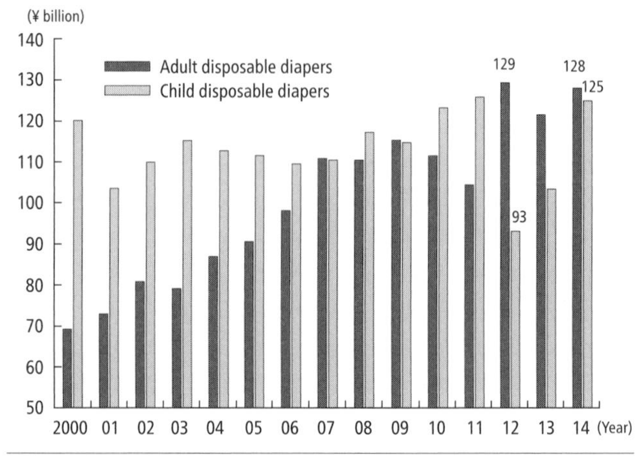

Source: Ministry of Economy, Trade and Industry, *Industrial Statistics*.

decline in the labor force, the number of commuters will top out and begin to decline. However, if high value-added services—that is, services with a high unit price per customer—are provided, sales revenues will not necessarily fall.

The few examples presented here are all product innovations that responded to social needs. You can see how they all created new growth from a different direction than the downward pressure of population.

Keynes' expectations for the future

The continuous introduction of new products and services makes our lives increasingly convenient. This generally brings about GDP growth. In fact, there is a high likelihood that the level of our welfare is actually higher than expressed by the GDP figures.

For example, regarding the convenience of illumination, the economist William Nordhaus calculated the price of the physical quantity of one lumen-hour of light starting from a candle (1827) through to the latest models of light bulbs in the 1990s. Nordhaus demonstrated that even though the true cost per lumen-hour had declined to 1/100th of its original price, the prices of the candles and light bulbs that generate illumination had conversely increased by eight times. In other words, the "true price" of illumination and the price index used as a statistic had diverged by 800 to 1 over 150 years. GDP is underestimating the improvement in our lives, at least as far as the value of illumination is concerned, to that extent.

As economic growth continues, how will our lives change in the future? In 1930, in the midst of the Great Depression, Keynes wrote an essay entitled "Economic Possibilities for Our Grandchildren" in which he discussed people's lives 100 years from then, in the early twenty-first century.

As the Great Depression was advancing before their eyes, many people thought the prosperity of the nineteenth century was a thing of the past and that the future was dark, or at least that the future of the British economy was bleak. Keynes began his essay by saying that view was entirely wrong.

He presented an optimistic forecast that technological improvements and capital accumulation would cause per capita income to steadily rise over the next 100 years to the beginning of the twenty-first century, and that people's standard of living would be far higher 100 years in the future than it was in the 1930s. He pointed out that, although the pace of technological progress had been surprisingly slow from earliest recorded history around 2000 B.C. to the early 1700s, the high-paced technological progress which began in the eighteenth century was poised to continue.

Keynes wrote that along with technological progress, capital accumulation would also continue. Here, what manifests great power is the interest rate. Once money is borrowed, the debt snowballs due to compound interest. The same holds true for the accumulation of assets. Because we have experienced many years of zero interest rates and live in an era where even negative interest rates have appeared, we tend to forget the power of the interest rate, but Thomas Piketty stressed that the accumulation of assets through interest brings about inequality. Keynes also emphasized the power of the interest rate throughout his career.

In his essay, Keynes used British foreign investment as an example to explain this point. According to Keynes, the balance of Britain's foreign assets in 1930, which amounted to about £4 billion, had originated with a sum of £40,000 from the treasure that Captain Francis Drake had stolen from Spain's "Invincible Armada" in 1580. These funds had increased at an annual rate of 3 percent and grown to £4 billion. That is the accumulation of capital. Even at an annual interest rate of 2 percent, capital will increase by 7.5 times over a period of 100 years.

Keynes projected that the standard of living in industrialized nations would improve by four to eight times over the next 100 years as a result of technological advances and the accumulation of capital, assuming there are no major wars and no explosive increase in the population. The outbreak of World War II in 1939, less than ten years after he wrote this essay, put the lie to one assumption, but still, the picture Keynes painted of the world 100 years in the future was an optimistic one.

Well, then, what did Keynes envision as the "wealthy society" 100 years in the future? He wrote that human beings have two types of needs. One is the need for essential goods and services we try to obtain regardless of other human beings' circumstances. The food needed to exist and a house for protection from rain and wind are representative of such items. The other is the need for goods and services we desire to make us feel superior to other human beings. Because they are relative, the demand for these goods can be considered unlimited. But leaving these aside, the demand for most goods and services gradually becomes saturated. Keynes predicted that, rather than making more and more goods and services, people would choose to spend their time and energy for purposes other than day-to-day life. In the world which Keynes expected 100 years into the future, it would be sufficient for people to work only five days a week and for just three hours a day.

Such a society would certainly give birth to boredom. Already in the 1920s, Keynes noted that there were wealthy ladies of leisure in Britain and the U.S. who had lost their purpose in life and fallen into boredom from having excessive amounts of money with too much free time. He discusses the "non-economic" purposes that humans should pursue to avoid such conditions. For Keynes, who associated with a collective of artists called the Bloomsbury Group in his youth, the answer was the arts. At any rate, Keynes predicted that in the wealthy society that would be realized in 100 years at the beginning of the twenty-first century, economics would become secondary for the first time in history, and the role of economists would become like that of dentists, and "that would be splendid." Keynes ends his essay with these words.

Keynes' predictions were incorrect. No one believes that a work schedule of three hours a day and fifteen hours a week will be realized easily now, or anytime soon. Poverty exists not only in developing countries, but in industrialized nations as well. Economics is still a significant issue for us today.

Mill's zero-growth theory

Contrary to Keynes' predictions, even though we have entered the twenty-first century, there are no signs that we have completely resolved all our economic problems. Nonetheless, if economic growth continues, we will someday achieve a society so wealthy that nothing further can be expected, which Keynes calls "economic bliss" in his essay. If that happens, then further economic growth will be unnecessary. The zero-growth society will have arrived.

The zero-growth theory has appeared repeatedly in history. In the world of economics, the argument developed in the nineteenth century by John Stuart Mill (1806–73) is well known. Mill, an intellectual giant of nineteenth-century England, is renowned for his treatise *On Liberty*. Mill's zero-growth theory appears in the chapter "Of the Stationary State" (book IV, chapter VI) of his *Principles of Political Economy*, which summarized classical economics from Adam Smith through to David Ricardo.

At the beginning of this short chapter of just six pages,

which follows a chapter that discusses economic growth and development, Mill raises the question of what goal society is moving toward with its economic growth and development. The leading economists of every era, starting with Adam Smith, have believed that economic growth and development are the basis of wealth. The understanding of economists was that, no matter how high the absolute level might become, wealth cannot be generated under zero growth. Yet even they would agree that economic growth cannot go on forever. At some point, we will have to settle into zero growth, that is, an economic stationary state.

Mill differs from other economists in that he did not view this stationary state as negative. He wrote that he detested a society where the call for growth and more growth has people pushing others aside in a competition to survive.

Mill's argument is reminiscent of the famous passage by Sōseki Natsume in his lecture "Gendai Nihon no kaika" (The civilization of modern-day Japan).

> In any case, we have these two intertwining processes, one involving inventions and mechanisms that spring from the desire to conserve our labor as much as possible, and the other involving amusements that spring from the wish to consume our energies as freely as possible. As the two intertwine like a textile's warp and woof, combining in infinitely varied ways, the result is this strange, chaotic phenomenon we know as our modern civilization.
>
> ... I said earlier that for all its progress, civilization favors us with so little peace of mind that, if we consider the added anxieties thrust on us by competition and the

> like, our happiness is probably not very different from what it was in the Stone Age.
>
> (translated by Jay Rubin)

What Sōseki calls "civilization" here generally corresponds to development of the economy.

Even if the economy develops and people's lives become more convenient, this does not necessarily mean that people will feel happy. Sōseki calls this "the great paradox to which civilization has given birth." He says that one reason for this is that, while Western civilization is "internally motivated," Japanese civilization is "externally motivated."

> A nation, a people, that incurs a civilization like this can only feel a sense of emptiness, of dissatisfaction and anxiety... This tells us that the civilization of modern-day Japan is superficial: it just skims the surface.
>
> (Ibid.)

Then, what should be done about this? In Japan, the following passage is well known.

> This is not to say that we must put a stop to it. There is really nothing we can do about it. We must go on skimming the surface, fighting back our tears.
>
> (Ibid.)

The theory of happiness of a stationary state

Let us return to Mill. He explained his own ideals as follows:

> The best state for human nature is that in which, while no one is poor, no one desires to be richer, nor has any reason

to fear being thrust back by the efforts of others to push themselves forward.

(*The Principles of Political Economy*)

Mill goes on to say that, while economic development is needed in poor developing countries, what is required in advanced countries such as England is not growth, but rather more equal distribution of income. Interestingly, he says strict population restrictions are indispensable for more equal income distribution, and that if population is allowed to increase freely, equal distribution of income cannot possibly be realized. On this point Mill is close to Malthus.

In industrialized nations, if there is technological progress, even if the population increases, the per capita income level may not have to decline. For example, economically a certain standard of living may be maintained by technological progress. Still, if the population increases, then the population density must inevitably also increase. In today's information society, where we are in constant contact with others through our mobile phones and e-mail, what Mill proceeds to say demands reflection.

It is not good for man to be kept perforce at all times in the presence of his species. A world from which solitude is extirpated, is a very poor ideal. Solitude, in the sense of being often alone, is essential to any depth of meditation or of character.

Mill acknowledges that economic growth inevitably alters nature, but he stresses the importance of leaving natural areas that are untouched. He presciently and poetically points to today's environmental problems. In this way, Mill says that, in advanced nations like Britain, a zero-growth society does not by any means cause poverty. On the contrary, he argues, a "stationary state" should bring people greater happiness than the single-minded pursuit of growth.

There are still persuasive arguments for zero-growth theory today, like that put forth by Mill. For example, from the perspective that economic growth alone is not the source of happiness and that resolving income inequality is more important, the economist Toshiaki Tachibanaki, who has conducted superior empirical research on income inequality and other issues in the Japanese economy, wrote the following while referring to Mill.

> Let us consider the zero-growth theory as it applies to contemporary Japan. The Japanese people have chosen lower birthrates over the past 20 or 30 years. This is causing a labor shortage and pushing down household consumption demand. So, we are choosing negative economic growth.
>
> Under these conditions, an economic growth strategy aiming at an annual growth rate of 2 to 3 percent is impossible. However, a negative growth rate would result in a declining standard of living, so I think that should be avoided. Accordingly, I approve a strategy to bring growth up to 0 percent.
>
> (Toshiaki Tachibanaki, *21 seiki no shihonshugi o yomitoku* [Analysis of twenty-first century capitalism])

Growth or equality?

Even looking only after World War II, this debate has taken place repeatedly ever since the high-growth era. Toward the end of the 1950s, when full-fledged high economic growth was about to begin, the debate between the economist Shigeto Tsuru and Hayato Ikeda, who ultimately put forth an "income-doubling plan" and became prime minister, was representative.

On top of his detailed criticism of Ikeda's concept, initially called the "monthly salary doubling theory," Tsuru wrote as follows.

> As you can understand from the above examination, the theoretical basis underpinning the bullishness of the "monthly salary doubling theory" is weak, and the practical problems for working to realize it are great. If the government takes active stimulus measures to unreasonably realize income doubling, that will potentially lead to inflation... Leaving the inflation problem aside, is 'income doubling' actually the primary problem?... In today's Japan, rather than raising income across the board, the greatest problem is to reduce the income gaps among various classes.
>
> ("Shotokubaizō wa hatashite kanō ka?" [Is income doubling actually feasible?], *Asahi Journal*, July 19, 1959).

Tsuru's argument is that the distribution of income is far more important than economic growth. Ikeda, who was then the Minister of International Trade and Industry in the Nobusuke Kishi administration, responded as follows.

The essay by Shigeto Tsuru in the July 19 edition of this magazine overlooks the big picture. His excessive inquisitiveness regarding trifles is a bit pitiful. It is not fundamentally important whether what doubles is gross income, per capita income, or monthly salaries. What is important is to strive as hard as possible to realize the doubling as quickly as possible...

As Tsuru points out, it is a fact that the Japanese economy has the problem of what is called a dual structure. However, this is the type of problem that can most smoothly and appropriately be resolved in the process of economic growth and development. Tsuru argues about the difficulty of reorganizing the industrial structure, but that is because he presumes a static economy. Changes in the industrial structure during periods of sudden expansion rapidly absorb the working population in growth sectors and rapidly advance by themselves.

The issue of reducing inequality is, of course, important. However, I do not agree with the way of thinking that has an undercurrent of the wartime emergency economic mentality or with the stationary feudalistic economy mentality which says "do not fear poverty, but fear inequality." Income gaps should be narrowed in the process of the economy expanding and total production increasing. In general, the problems with economic growth should be understood and resolved in a dynamic development process incidentally including the so-called dual-structure problem.

("Bokkōki ni aru Nihon keizai" [The Japanese economy in a period of sudden expansion], *Asahi Journal*, August 2, 1959)

Is economic growth necessary?

The issue of growth or equality has been examined repeatedly. The question "Is economic growth necessary?" is examined in the Afterword added to the paperback edition of my book *Kōdo seichō: Nihon o kaeta 6,000 nichi* [High growth: 6,000 days that changed Japan], and some of the contents here will overlap with those, but in this book I want to finally reconsider this question one more time.

When Japan's high-growth period ended just forty years ago, society began to question economic growth, which had been viewed as self-evident up until that time. The report issued by the Club of Rome explaining the restrictions on economic growth under a limited global environment truly marked the changing of the era. For the forty years since then, there has been an ongoing underlying sentiment in society that economics is a somewhat suspicious presence.

When "market fundamentalism" is mentioned, one imagines a cold-blooded, inhuman social mechanism. Accidents have occurred when priority is given to economic efficiency. In 2008, tens of millions of innocent people lost their jobs worldwide in the financial crisis following the bankruptcy of Lehman Brothers and the collapse of a bubble economy that was sparked by greedy capitalism. Economic growth has come to represent economic supremacism, whose role has ended. Keishi Saeki may have spoken the feelings of a great many Japanese in his comments following the experience of the Tōhoku earthquake and tsunami of March 11, 2011. "The ruthless ferocity of nature has cut a deep wound in the spirit of the Japanese people. Many people may have changed their views on life and death and on nature. Postwar

Japanese values and the sense of happiness from increasing production, gaining wealth, and becoming free has collapsed and disappeared" (*Yomiuri Shimbun*, December 17, 2011).

In fact, such feelings did not first emerge in the period from the latter half of the twentieth century through the beginning of the twenty-first century. I have already explained Mill's "zero-growth theory." Prior to that, the new intellectual movement of Romanticism in Europe at the beginning of the nineteenth century was fundamentally "anti-economic"—the antithesis of capitalism, which was poised for a meteoric rise. If one looks for it, this sort of sentiment can easily be found in both the East and the West.

At the 2012 U.N. General Assembly, in front of representatives gathered from 188 nations worldwide, the president of Uruguay, José Mujica, who gained attention as the world's poorest president, said, "A poor person is not someone who has little, but one who needs infinitely more, and more and more." Such words strike a chord in people's hearts.

The history of humanity might even be seen as a history of the conflict between what I would term the philosophy of Romanticism—which turns its back on economics—and rationalism, which criticizes it.

"Their food is plain and good, their clothing fine but simple, their homes secure, they are happy in their ways." The philosophy of Lao Tzu—who thinks people should come to know their lots in nature, see current conditions as good, and not seek much in vain—and who advocates doing nothing and taking things as they come, is of course anti-growth and anti-economics. Many people also sense that the pursuit of economic growth is originally a Western concept, while

Eastern philosophy as represented by Lao Tzu sees "not to desire" as ideal.

The benefits of economic growth

There are great differences between Eastern and Western philosophy, but the situation is not all that simple. That is because the way of thinking represented by Lao Tzu is harshly criticized by Confucianism, which may be considered the leading Eastern philosophy. The *Yuan Dao* (which means the "True Path"), written by the Tang Confucian scholar Han Yu, is a representative example. "In ancient times, people faced many perils." This means that in ancient times, the environment surrounding human beings was harsh. The individuals who improved this in a visible manner were called sages. "When it became cold, they discovered how to make clothing; when the people were hungry, they discovered how to make food. They also started medicine and saved people from early death."

The Japanese Sinologist Konan Naitō explained this as follows.

> When authors are called sages in China, this refers to those who made various work tools for people and for their lives, and who further created the rules of civilization; sages from Fuxi and Shennong to King Wu and the Duke of Zhou are all that type of people.
>
> (Torajirō Konan Naitō, *Zōho: Nihonbunkashi kenkyū* [Enlarged edition: Japanese cultural history research])

In the West as well, in the seventeenth century, Thomas Hobbes (1588–1679) proclaimed the natural state of the life of man as "nasty, brutish, and short."

Would those who rail against the economy and modernity actually refuse antibiotics if they themselves became ill? The number of dead and missing in the Isewan Typhoon of 1959 exceeded 5,000 people. Typhoons today do not cause that many fatalities. At such times, we first come to know the value of civilization. What Lao Tzu advocated cannot be practical theory; this is what Han Yu explains. Many people may view Confucianism as antiquated, but on the contrary, at its base is a clear "rationalism" that completely differs from Lao Tzu. The person referred to as a "sage" in Confucianism could be termed an innovator—that is, one who implements innovation, which is viewed by Schumpeter as the fundamental force that moves capitalism. In this way, Confucianism (including the neo-Confucianism which was a mainstay for the samurai for 300 years in the Edo period) is clearly pro-economics.

Of course, I am not attempting to advocate economic growth above all by citing Confucianism as a reference. Now that the sustainability of the global environment is being questioned, there will no longer be anyone who advocates the supremacy of economic growth for its own sake. But forgetting the fruits of economic growth and carelessly arguing against growth is dangerous.

For example, I think glorifying the Edo period, which was a period of low growth, as a sustainable and stable society is entirely too one-sided. There may well have been many good aspects to the Edo period, but I find the newspaper article

"Conditions during the Edo Period as Told by Bones" more convincing and real. This article explains that human bones excavated during development projects in Tokyo are preserved in large numbers at the National Museum of Nature and Science. These are the remains of roughly 10,000 people. Their bones convey the living conditions of people during the Edo period, and indicate that nutritional conditions were poor, with a shortage of iron in particular. One characteristic is the large number of bones of younger people, who have low mortality rates today. The remains tell us that there were frequent epidemics of infectious diseases and that people died easily. The average height of an adult male was around 155 centimeters, and women were about 10 centimeters shorter, making them the shortest in all Japanese history. Experts say that, in addition to the poor nutritional conditions, the people may have suffered stress from living close together in cramped row houses. "Living conditions were harsh. The bones bear a record of the shadow side of the Edo period, which would better be called a slum." (*Asahi Shimbun*, December 17, 2011, evening edition).

As we have already seen, there are some economists who advocate the zero-growth theory. But comparing the actual conditions during the Edo period with those of today, it might be better for us to more frankly appreciate the benefits of economic growth.

The role of entertainment

Sombart's theory that "luxury" is the source that generates economic growth in the first place is introduced above. While excessive luxury cannot be called a virtue, Sōseki already noted 100 years ago that there is no point to denying luxury unconditionally. The *Civilization of Modern-Day Japan*, quoted above, includes the following passage.

> In plain language, people become extravagant. From an ethical perspective, Taoists warn against perpetual luxury. That is certainly good advice, but since it is an admonishment against the natural general tendency, it ultimately winds up failing. If you think about how extravagant human beings have become from ancient times up to today, this is understandable.

Of course, there is meaningless luxury that should be rejected; that would certainly be recognized by Sōseki as well. For example, it is said that an elevator made of gold was once fabricated in a Middle Eastern country that had become wealthy from oil revenues. This is a ridiculous idea, and everyone would surely agree that no economic growth would be better than economic growth for such purposes.

Though such absurdity may have emerged at times, the question is: what have the 250 years of economic growth since the eighteenth century brought about for human beings? What is the essence of the intertwining processes that Sōseki referred to, "one involving inventions and mechanisms that spring from the desire to conserve our labor as much as possible, and the other involving amusements that spring from the wish to consume our energies as freely as possible"?

We all know that entertainment is not conducted for any rational purpose. For human beings with developed brains, entertainment and play perform the essential roles noted in *Homo Ludens* by the Dutch Historian Johan Huizinga, who is best known for his masterpiece *The Autumn of the Middle Ages*. However, one look at a kitten playing with a ball of yarn shows that enjoying entertainment is not the exclusive purview of human beings.

The limits and lifespans of innovations

Leaving "entertainment" aside, the issue becomes the effect of what Sōseki called "[a process] involving inventions and mechanisms that spring from the desire to conserve our labor as much as possible." Of course, such goods and services directly generate convenience. But upon careful reflection, we cannot help but notice how such goods and services have ultimately contributed to increasing human life expectancy.

These goods and services include medical technology and pharmaceuticals, as well as highly nutritious foods. Yet those are by no means the only items that contribute to increasing the average lifespan. On cold winter nights, high-quality housing with well-insulated walls and windows that block the north wind have contributed to lowering the mortality rates of infants and the elderly. The development of various means of transportation has not only enabled the entertainment of sightseeing trips to distant locations, but it has also clearly contributed to the extension of our average life expectancy, because without them we would have to expend a great deal of energy in walking every day. The same can be said of elevators and escalators.

As I have written repeatedly, what drives economic

growth in developed nations is product innovation. Many of the new goods and services created by product innovation are believed to have contributed to increasing average life expectancy in a roundabout way. As I mentioned before, this is exactly what Han Yu pointed out in the ancient Tang dynasty. In every era, the larger average income realized as a result of economic growth has made it possible for people to purchase such new goods and services. Thus, average life expectancy has increased in the industrialized nations, contrary to the projections by Malthus.

Thinking in this way, one might say that whether economic growth is now unnecessary in industrialized nations ultimately depends on whether we think the average life expectancy is sufficient, and does not have to be extended further now that it has surpassed eighty years.

To be certain, an average life expectancy of more than eighty years may be coming up against biological limitations. In his books *Zō no jikan nezumi no jikan* (Elephant time and mouse time) and *Seibutsugakuteki bunmeiron* (Biological theory of civilization), the biologist Tatsuo Motokawa speaks about the lifespans of animals. He says that all animals, be they mice or elephants, die after their hearts beat around 1.5 billion times. However, the amount of time it takes for one heartbeat is longer for heavier animals. The heartbeat of an elephant that weighs three tons takes eighteen times longer than that of a mouse weighing 30 grams. That is, the elephant's heart beats more slowly. Now, because the number of heartbeats until death is still 1.5 billion in either case, the lifespan of the mouse is two or three years while the lifespan of the elephant is seventy years. But what about human beings? Human beings are just forty-two years old when their hearts have beat 1.5 billion times! If this is the natural average life expectancy of human beings from a biological perspective, then the average life expectancy in industrialized nations is approaching twice its natural length.

If average life expectancies are approaching biological limits in industrialized nations, the return on product innovation may gradually decline over the long term. In fact, since the start of the 2010s, the growth of productivity has declined noticeably—even in the U.S., which has led the global economy for 100 years, since the start of the twentieth century. There is now an active debate as to whether the world has entered an era of long stagnation. The abnormally low interest rates, which are historically unprecedented (as of July 2016, the interest rates on ten-year government bonds are 1.42 percent in the U.S., −0.023 percent in Germany, and −0.225 percent in Japan), signal that people are sensing the arrival of a long-term recession.

The future of the Japanese economy

Finally, let us consider the future of the Japanese economy. After the postwar recovery and the subsequent high-growth era came to an end and we entered the 1970s, the drive for growth at all costs disappeared. For industrialized nations, this is an inevitability of history. But it is different from the zero-growth theory in the literal sense. For humans, rather than remaining static in one place forever, it is more comfortable for everyone to move at their own pace. For mature industrialized nations as well, economic growth that matches each economy is far more natural than zero growth. Under zero growth, the employment conditions of the working generation, especially of youth, inevitably degrade. From that perspective as well, economic growth is necessary after all.

Japan's average life expectancy of 80.5 years for men and 86.8 years for women (2015) may well be approaching the physiological limits. Yet the issues of healthy life expectancy and quality of life still remain. Even if the twenty-first century does not see the type of average life expectancy gains that were achieved in industrialized nations in the twentieth century, massive product innovations are still necessary so that people can live comfortably in the super-aged society that is already emerging. In this society, it is not only medicine and nursing care that will have to change but everything from housing, transportation, distribution, and even writing instruments to entire cities. Like it or not, this can only be realized through economic growth. This kind of innovation is the wellspring of economic growth in industrialized nations.

Japan's labor force peaked at 67.93 million people in 1998, shifting into decline about ten years before the population began to fall. There were years after that when the labor force increased from the greater participation of women in the labor market, but over the long term the labor force will continue declining at an annual rate of around 0.6 percent.

Many economists say that Japan's potential growth rate is only around 0.5 percent, but I believe Japan has the potential for real economic growth at a pace of around 1.5 percent. That would require labor productivity growth of around 2 percent. If that can be achieved, then per capita GDP and per capita income will grow at an annual rate of around 2 percent, and will therefore double in thirty-five years. Consequently, the lifetime income of those who are presently thirty years old should grow to twice that of those who are now sixty-five years old.

What are the present conditions of labor productivity in Japan? Looking at the trend over the fourteen years from 2000 through 2014—excluding 2009, when negative growth of 5.5 percent was recorded in the worldwide Great Recession immediately following the bankruptcy of Lehman Brothers—the average annual rate of decline in the labor force was 0.2 percent. On the other hand, the average annual economic growth rate over the same fourteen years was 1.3 percent. Despite all the talk about how bad the economy was, labor productivity rose at an annual rate of 1.5 percent. So, 2.0 percent is by no means an impossible number.

When innovation is mentioned among people who know economics, many see it is as only affecting the supply side of the economy, that is, as a supply-side phenomenon. The concept of the "potential growth rate," which may be called the "capacity" of the economy, also follows the standard supply-side method of compiling how much labor and capital can increase in the future. Innovation, however—especially product innovation that creates new goods and services—is closely related to demand, as explained in detail in this chapter.

The problem is whether Japanese enterprises can achieve the product innovation required to respond to the potential demand. There is a high likelihood that, in thirty-five years, Japanese people may have double the purchasing power we have now. What types of goods and services will the future Japanese seek to buy with their strong purchasing power?

No one can accurately envision the coming super-aged society. But there is no doubt that the changes that occur will be so great that they will transform all of society. These will be realized by countless innovations, small and large. It is no exaggeration to say that the Japanese economy, which has a high income level and a large market, and is facing above all the issue of the super-aged society, presents Japanese enterprises with an ideal proving ground. We often hear that there is no future for the market inside Japan, where the population is shrinking, but the Japanese economy has huge hidden potential for innovation toward the super-aged society.

We must understand how, in the super-aged society, the elderly in fact require a great many goods and services. Many people believe that consumption is primarily carried out by the working-age generation, and consumption by the elderly is limited. The assertion that consumption will not increase in Japan because the working-age segment of the population (fifteen to sixty-four years old) is going to decline is based on that kind of thinking.

People who accept this idea may have something like a ramen-eating contest in mind when they are thinking about consumption. Naturally, in that kind of setting, seniors in their seventies cannot possibly compete with youth in their twenties. But this is absolutely the wrong paradigm for understanding the consumption patterns of persons in different age groups.

To examine this, let us analyze the scale of consumption related to the elderly.

Although we speak about "household consumption" as a single concept, looking in detail, the items that are consumed differ for each age group. That is no surprise. But even though the goods and services purchased differ, the real question is the amount of goods and services that are purchased—that is, consumed—by each age group. In this regard, the key point is purchasing power. Regardless of how much a consumer may want something, without sufficient purchasing power, that desire will not result in actual consumption.

The sources of purchasing power differ greatly between the working-age generation and the elderly. For most working-age people, the wages and income they gain from their labor constitute the foundation of their economic strength. In contrast, those sixty-five and older have little labor income. If they are retired, it amounts to absolutely nothing. Aside from monthly pensions, dividends (though interest is virtually zero at present), etc., the pillar of the economic power of the elderly is their assets, which are the result of the savings they accumulated during their working years. In fact, the majority of all assets are owned by the elderly.

Chart 4-5 presents the changes in the total amounts of financial assets held by each age group from 1989 to 2014. As you can see, over the past twenty-plus years, the financial assets held by those sixty and older have increased remarkably. This, of course, is a consequence of the aging of society. As of 2014, out of the ¥1,700 trillion in financial assets held by individuals, approximately ¥1,000 trillion, or 60 percent, is held by persons sixty and older.

Now, let us perform some simple calculations to see just how much purchasing power the elderly have. First, we'll assume that sixty-five is the average age of those in their sixties and that seventy-five is the average age of those in their

Chart 4-5. Total Amounts of Financial Assets Held by Age Segment

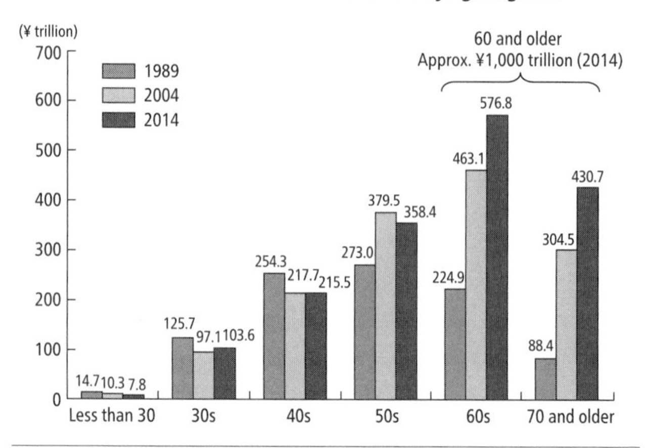

Source: October 27, 2015, Ministry of Finance, Tax Commission.

seventies. Next, we'll assume that each individual will live until eighty-five, which is roughly the same as the current life expectancy (eighty-one for men, eighty-seven for women). While most of the elderly leave behind some sort of financial assets, looking at the most recent Cabinet Office survey (chart 4-6), the elderly mostly save money to support themselves in their old age, and only a few (2.6 percent) desire to leave large financial assets behind for their children. Here, for simplicity's sake, let us assume that the elderly use up all their financial assets. This means that those who are sixty-five use up all their financial assets over twenty years and those who are seventy-five use them up over ten years until they pass away at age eighty-five. If they use equal amounts of their financial assets each year, then the annual consumption of those in their sixties becomes 1/20 of their financial assets

Chart 4-6. Purposes of Savings

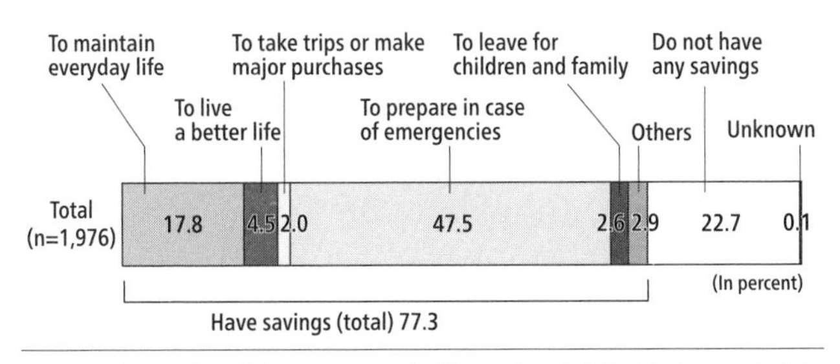

Source: Cabinet Office, "2016 Survey on the Economic and Living Environment of the Elderly."

of ¥580 trillion; that is, ¥29 trillion. The annual consumption of those seventy or older becomes 1/10 of their financial assets of ¥430 trillion, or ¥43 trillion, making a total of ¥72 trillion per year. These calculations assume that the elderly use up all their financial assets by the time they pass away. Even if we assume that they leave behind 20 percent for their children, the total annual consumption generated by seniors sixty and older from using their assets for themselves would be 80 percent of ¥72 trillion; that is, ¥58 trillion.

Japan's GDP is presently on the order of ¥500 trillion, of which household consumption comprises around ¥300 trillion. This shows how large annual consumption of ¥58 trillion generated by the assets of the elderly would be. Of course, this ¥58 trillion figure simply shows the *potential* purchasing power that the elderly have, should they decide to consume. Whether or not they actually consume is a different issue.

In practice, there are two main factors that prevent the elderly from consuming to the point that they decrease their assets. The first is anxiety about the future, due to not knowing how much money will be required for medical and nursing care in the years ahead. The Cabinet Office survey in chart 4-6 indicates that "to prepare in case of emergencies" is the top purpose cited for savings by the elderly. The second factor limiting consumption is the lack of goods and services that the elderly feel they really want to buy.

Let me now advance the concept of "age-nomics," which is the single clue to resolving both these issues. It is the key that will open the safe containing the nearly ¥60 trillion per year in purchasing power held by Japan's senior citizens.

If the markets for the goods and services the elderly seek expand, then the economic growth rate will, of course, increase by that amount. Japan's GDP is ¥500 trillion; 1 percent of GDP is ¥5 trillion. Therefore, if 10 percent of the potential purchasing power held by the elderly were converted to actual consumption, Japan's growth rate would rise by 1 percent every year. As stated earlier, the greatest factor restricting economic growth in industrialized countries is the saturation of demand for existing goods and services. Businesses seek to produce new goods, but they do not know what to produce. Age-nomics is the answer to that question.

Age-nomics places the focus on the goods and services that the elderly require. However, its benefits by no means accrue to the elderly alone.

Let us assume that age-nomics succeeds, and that the Japanese economy grows at an annual rate of 1.5 percent. That is equal to Japan's actual growth rate since the start of the twenty-first century. The growth rates being assumed by European countries, whose economies are more mature than Japan's, are a bit higher than this (and the rate assumed by the U.S. is higher still). Japan's population will decline by 0.5 percent per year, so if the GDP grows by 1.5 percent per year, per capita income will rise by around 2.0 percent (1.5 percent minus negative 0.5 percent) per year. Because a growth rate of 2.0 percent per year results in a doubling over 35 years, the lifetime income of those who are presently 30 years old should end up being twice that of the baby-boom generation.

With the continued aging of society, the percentage of consumers who are elderly will rise more and more over the twenty-first century. It is age-nomics that holds the key to both a rich life for the elderly in their old age and to the life of those in the working-age generation.

Chart 4-7. Changes in the Savings and Investment Differential by Sector (versus GDP ratio)

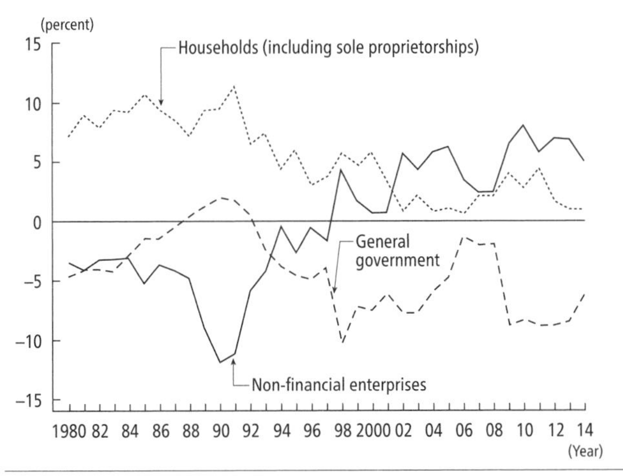

Source: Cabinet Office, *Annual Report on National Accounts*, net lending (+) or net borrowing (−) by institutional sector.

Note: 2000 base from 1980 through 1993, 2005 base from 1994.

Unfortunately, Japanese firms presently lack initiative. Chart 4-7 presents the change in savings—that is, the difference between earnings and expenditures—by household, corporations, government entities, etc. The corporate sector has now surpassed households to become the largest net saver in Japan. Can this not be called the naked state of capitalism?

In the past, households maintained savings and corporations made investments with negative savings; that is, with borrowings. Corporations say that the times have changed, but what has changed is not the times, but the corporations.

Schumpeter emphasized that, beyond financial return, the essential driver of innovation for entrepreneurs is the realization of their own vision toward the future. Keynes also said that corporate capital investment is ultimately a result of "animal spirits" like those that inspired Roald Amundsen to take off with dog sleds toward the South Pole. Consequently, Keynes said, enterprises that lose healthy optimism and rely on nothing but rational calculations will fade and die.

Ultimately, the future of the Japanese economy depends on whether Japanese enterprises can conquer population-decline pessimism.

Afterword

The preliminary results of the *2015 Population Census of Japan*, which is conducted once every five years, were announced this June. They showed that the aging of society and the declining birthrate had progressed a step further in comparison to the previous census in 2010. The percentage of people in the total population who were at least sixty-five years old was 26.7 percent, surpassing one out of every four people for the first time. This was higher than the 22.4 percent in Italy and the 21.2 percent in Germany, though both of those societies are aging rapidly, and the highest among the leading industrialized nations. Meanwhile, the percentage of the Japanese population under the age of fifteen posted a historical low of 12.7 percent. In Japan, the number of children is now less than half the number of senior citizens.

The population of Japan is decreasing amid these trends. If no measures are taken, the current population of 127.11 million is projected to decline to 81 million in 2065. The government has therefore presented a target of maintaining a population of 100 million. Childcare support that makes childbirth and childrearing easier is certainly important, but even if the birthrate rises, by itself that will not be sufficient to realize a population of 100 million in 2065. Because the number of young women in Japan has shrunk too far, even if the number of children that each woman gives birth to increases, it is already becoming impossible to stop the trend of population decline.

If the Japanese government were serious about stopping a decline in population, the decisive measure would be to accept immigrants, as Germany has chosen to do. There is a lot of argument about the acceptance of immigrants, although that topic is not addressed at all in this book. Regardless, the latest archeological and anthropological research makes clear that various peoples migrated to the Japanese archipelago through diverse routes from the north and from the south. Since recorded history as well, many migrants (naturalized citizens) brought advanced civilization from the continent to Japan, as we learn in history class at school. I think that Japanese who live in the twenty-first century need to look once more at the makeup of our country.

The decline of population is a major problem for Japan, as seen in chapter 2, but the argument that economic growth is impossible because the population is shrinking is not correct. That is what I have repeatedly written in this book. Now is the time we want to remember the role of innovation expounded by Schumpeter.

While this is a small and humble book, I have received assistance from a great many people in its preparation. I had the opportunity to participate in a conference called "The Future We Choose" at the Cabinet Office in 2014, and I would like to note here that I learned a great deal during those discussions.

In particular, I want to thank Shūko Miyagawa from my office for preparing all of the materials for this publication. I also want to thank Masatoshi Tanaka of the Chuokoron-Shinsha editorial department for his many insightful comments. I would like to express my sincere gratitude to both of them.

The writing of this book has been a milestone for me as a scholar since I retired from the University of Tokyo, where I taught for nearly 30 years. In closing, I would like to dedicate this English edition as a gift to my wife Setsuko, with whom I celebrated our fortieth wedding anniversary last year, and to my daughter Momoko and her husband Takashi, who are starting out on their new life together.

July 10, 2016
Hiroshi Yoshikawa

Bibliography

Anderson, Michael. *Population Change in North-Western Europe, 1750–1850*. London: Macmillan Education Ltd., 1988.

Aoki, Kazuo. *Nihon no rekishi 3: Nara no Miyako* [Japanese history 3: The Nara capital]. Tokyo: Chuokoronsha, 1965.

Brentano, L. "The Doctrine of Malthus and the Increase of Population During the Last Decades." *Economic Journal* 20, no. 79 (1910): 371–93.

Brynjolfsson, Erik. and Andrew McAfee. *Race Against the Machine*. Tennessee: Lightning Source, Inc., 2011.

Cabinet Office. *Sentaku suru mirai: Jinkō suikei kara mietekuru miraizō* [The future we choose: Image of the future seen from population estimates]. Tokyo: Nikkei Printing, 2015.

Darwin, Charles. *On the Origin of Species by Means of Natural Selection, or the Preservation of Favoured Races in the Struggle for Life*. London: John Murray, 1859.

Deaton, A. *The Great Escape: Health, Wealth, and the Origins of Inequality*. New Jersey: Princeton University Press, 2013.

Engel, Ernst. *Die Lebenskosten belgischer Arbeiter-Familien früher und jetzt* [The cost of living of Belgian working families then and now]. Dresden: Heinrich, 1895.

Fisher, J. C. and R. H. Pry. "A Simple Substitution Model of Technological Change." *Technological Forecasting and Social Change* 3 (1971): 75–88.

Fogel, R. *The Escape from Hunger and Premature Death, 1700–2100: Europe, America, and the Third World*. Cambridge: Cambridge University Press, 2004.

Fujita, Nanako. *Myurudāru no keizaigaku* [Myrdal's economics]. Tokyo: NTT Publishing, 2010.

Hasegawa, Mariko. "Shinka seibutsugaku kara mita shōshika: Hito dake ga naze tokushu nanoka?" [The declining birth rate as seen from evolutionary biology: Why are only humans unique?]. *Gakushikai Kaihō* no. 915, 2015-4 (November 2015): 71–78.

Hirooka, Masaaki. *Gijutsu kakushin to keizai hatten* [Technological innovation and economic development]. Tokyo: Nikkei Inc., 2003.

Ho, Ping-ti. *Studies on the Population of China, 1368–1953*. Cambridge, MA: Harvard University Press, 1959.

Huizinga, J. *Homo Ludens: Proeve Ener Bepaling van het Spelelement der Cultuur* [Homo ludens: A study of the play-element in culture]. Groningen: Wolters-Noordhoff, 1938.

Ihara, Hiroshi and Hiroshi Umemura. *Sekai no rekishi 7: Sō to Chūō Yūrashia* [World history 7: The Song Dynasty and Central Eurasia]. Tokyo: Chuokoronsha, 1997.

Johanson, S. R. and C. Mosk. "Exposure, Resistance and Life Expectancy: Disease and Death during the Economic Development of Japan, 1900–1960." *Population Studies* 41 (1987): 207–23.

Katō, Shigeru. *Shina keizaishi gaisetsu* [Outline of Chinese economic history]. Tokyo: Kobundo Shobo, 1944.

Keynes, J. M. "Alfred Marshall, 1842–1924." In *The Collected Writings of John Maynard Keynes, vol. X: Essays in Biography*. London: Royal Economic Society, 1924.

———. *The Economic Consequences of the Peace*. London: Macmillan, 1919. Reprinted as *The Collected Writings of John Maynard Keynes, vol. 2: The Economic Consequences of the Peace*. London: Royal Economic Society, 1978.

———. "Economic Possibilities for Our Grandchildren." In *The Collected Writings of John Maynard Keynes, vol. 9: Essays in Persuasion*. London: Royal Economic Society, 1930.

———. *The General Theory of Employment, Interest and Money*. London: Macmillan, 1936.

———. "Some Economic Consequences of a Declining Population." In *The Collected Writings of John Maynard Keynes, vol. 14: The General Theory and After: Part 2, Defence and Development*. London: Royal Economic Society, 1937.

Kitō, Hiroshi. *Jinkō kara yomu Nihon no rekishi* [A view of Japanese history through population]. Tokyo: Kodansha, 2000.

Livi-Bacci, Massimo. *A Concise History of World Population*, 5th ed. Chichester: Wiley-Blackwell, 2012.

Maddison, A. *Monitoring the World Economy 1820–1992*. Paris: OECD, 1995.

Malthus, T. R. *An Essay on the Principle of Population*. London: J. Johnson, 1798.

Mandeville, B. *The Fable of the Bees*. London: J. Tonson. 1714.

Masuda, Hiroya. *Chihō shōmetsu* [The disappearance of the regions]. Tokyo: Chuokoron-Shinsha, 2014.

Minami, Ryōshin. *Nihon no keizai hatten* [Japan's economic development]. Tokyo: Toyo Keizai Inc., 2002.

Motokawa, Tatsuo. *Seibutsugakuteki bunmeiron* [Biological theory of civilization]. Tokyo: Shinchosha, 2011.

———. *Zō no jikan nezumi no jikan* [Elephant time and mouse time]. Tokyo: Chuokoron-Shinsha, 1992.

Murakawa, Kentarō. "Girisha no suitai ni tsuite" [On the decline of Greece]. In *Sekai no rekishi dai 6 kan* [World history vol. 6]. Tokyo: Mainichi Shimbun, 1954; reprinted in *Murakawa Kentarō kodaishi ronshū 1*, [Collection of essays on ancient history by Kentarō Murakawa, vol. 1]. Tokyo: Iwanami Shoten, 1986.

Myrdal, Gunnar. "Population Problems and Policies." *The Annals of the American Academy of Political and Social Science*, vol. 197 (May 1938): 200–215.

Nakaya, Ukichirō. "Rōreigaku: Nagaiki o suru gakumon no sonzai" [Gerontology: Existence of the science of longevity]. In *Hanamizuki* [Dogwood]. Tokyo: Bungei Shunju Shinsha, 1950; reprinted in *Nakaya Ukichirō zuihitsu senshū dai 2 kan* [Collected essays of Ukichirō Nakaya, vol. 2]. Tokyo: Asahi Shimbunsha, 1966.

Natsume, Sōseki. *Nikki* [Diary], 1901. Reprinted in *Sōseki zenshū dai 13 kan* [Collected works of Sōseki, vol. 13]. Tokyo: Iwanami Shoten, 1966.

Negishi, Tatsuo and Masako Naitō. "Genjō to sono haikei kara mita 21 seiki no iryō seido" [The twenty-first century medical system seen from its current conditions and their background]. In *Iryō no keizaigakuteki bunseki* [Economic analysis of healthcare], edited by Hirofumi Uzawa. Tokyo: Nippon Hyoronsha, 1987.

Nordhaus, W. "Traditional Productivity Estimates Are Asleep at the (Technological) Switch." *Economic Journal* (September 1997): 1548–1559.

Ogura, Seiritsu and Reiko Suzuki. "Wagakuni sengoki (1950 nen kara 1965 nen) ni okeru nyūji shibōritsu no teika" [The decline of the infant mortality rate in Japan in the postwar era (1950–1965)]. In *Nichibei iryō shisutemu no hikaku kenkyū (jō)* [Comparative research on the Japanese and U.S. medical systems (1)]. Tokyo: National Institute for Research Advancement, 1993.

Ōuchi, Hyōe, Hiromi Arisawa, Yoshitarō Wakimura, and Ryōkichi Minobe. *Nihon keizai zusetsu* [The Japanese economy illustrated]. Tokyo: Iwanami Shinsho, 1955.

Peltzman, S. "Mortality Inequality." *Journal of Economic Perspectives* 23, no. 4 (2009): 175–190.

Petty, William. *Political Arithmetick*. London: Robert Clavel, Hen. Mortlock, 1690.

Piketty, T. *Capital in the Twenty-First Century*. Cambridge, MA: Harvard University Press, 2014.

Robertson, D. H. "The World Slump." In *Economic Essays and Addresses*, edited by A. C. Pigou and D. H. Robertson. London: P. S. King & Son, 1931.

Samuelson, P. "Ricardo was Right!" *Scandinavian Journal of Economics* 91, no. 1 (1989): 47–62.

Sawada, Goichi. *Nara Chō jidai minsei keizai no sūteki kenkyū* [Numerical study of the economy under the civil administration in the Nara period]. Tokyo: Fuzambo, 1927. Republished by Kashiwa Shobo, 1972.

Schumpeter, Joseph A. *History of Economic Analysis*. New York: Oxford University Press, 1954.

Shakespeare, William. *King Lear*. London: Nathaniel Butter, 1608.

Smith, Adam. *An Inquiry into the Nature and Causes of the Wealth of Nations*. London: W. Stahan, T. Cadell, 1776.

Sombart, W. *Liebe, Luxus und Kapitalismus* [Love, luxury and capitalism]. München, Leipzig: Duncker & Humblot, 1912.

Tachibanaki, Toshiaki. *21 seiki no shihonshugi o yomitoku* [Analysis of twenty-first century capitalism]. Tokyo: Takarajimasha, 2015.

"Tokushū: Jumyō" [Special feature: Lifespan]. *Kagaku* [Science] (December 2004): 1389–1447.

Tominaga, Kenichi. *Nihon no kindaika to shakai hendō* [Modernization and social change in Japan]. Tokyo: Kodansha, 1990.

Toye, J. *Keynes on Population*. New York: Oxford University Press, 2000.

Tsuchiya, Takao. *Kinsei Nihon: Hōkenshakai no shiteki bunseki* [Premodern Japan: Historical analysis of feudal society]. Tokyo: Ochanomizu Shobo, 1949.

Ueda, Masao, Atsushi Shimokōbe, Tomio Fumoto and Yūzō Morita. "Shinshun zadankai: Jinkō kara mita Nihon no genjō to shōrai" [New Year's roundtable: Japan's present and future conditions from the viewpoint of population]. *Tokei* (January 1967): 1–10.

Weil, D. "A Review of Angus Deaton's *The Great Escape: Health, Wealth, and the Origins of Inequality*," *Journal of Economic Literature 2015* 53, no. 1 (2015): 102–114.

Wicksell, Knut. *Föreläsningar i nationalekonomi*. Stockholm: Fritze, 1901. Translated by E. Claassen as *Lectures on Political Economy* (New York: George Routledge & Sons, 1934–35).

Yoshikawa, Hiroshi. *Kōdo seichō: Nihon o kaeta 6,000 nichi* [High growth: 6,000 days that changed Japan]. Tokyo: Chuokoron-Shinsha, 2012.

Hiroshi Yoshikawa

Hiroshi Yoshikawa is the president of Rissho University. He was born in Tokyo in 1951, received his B.A. from the University of Tokyo Faculty of Economics and his Ph.D. from Yale University, and subsequently taught as an assistant professor at the State University of New York (Albany), an associate professor at the Institute of Social and Economic Research at Osaka University, an associate professor at the University of Tokyo, and a professor at the University of Tokyo Graduate School of Economics. Yoshikawa specializes in macroeconomics and the Japanese economy.

His publications include *Macro-Econophysics* (Cambridge University Press, 2017, with Hideaki Aoyama, Yoshi Fujiwara, Yuichi Ikeda, Hiroshi Iyetomi, and Wataru Souma); *Defurēshon* [Deflation] (Nikkei Publishing Inc., 2013); *Japan's Lost Decade*, revised and expanded edition (I-House Press, 2008); *Reconstructing Macroeconomics: A Perspective from Statistical Physics and Combinatorial Stochastic Processes* (Cambridge University Press, 2007, with Masanao Aoki); and *Macroeconomics and the Japanese Economy* (Oxford University Press, 1995).

（英文版）人口と日本経済　長寿、イノベーション、経済成長
Population and the Japanese Economy: Longevity, Innovation, and Economic Growth

---

2020年3月27日　第1刷発行

著　者　　吉川　洋
訳　者　　チャールズ・スチュワート
発行所　　一般財団法人出版文化産業振興財団
〒101-0051 東京都千代田区神田神保町2-2-30
電話　03-5211-7283
ホームページ　https://www.jpic.or.jp/

印刷・製本所　　大日本印刷株式会社

定価はカバーに表示してあります。

Printed in Japan
ISBN 978-4-86658-056-2

OHIO NORTHERN UNIVERSITY
3 5111 00683 1667